AF412560

THE
POLITICAL
CAREER
OF
PETER PAUL RUBENS

THIS IS THE SEVENTH OF THE

WALTER NEURATH MEMORIAL LECTURES

WHICH ARE GIVEN ANNUALLY EACH SPRING ON

SUBJECTS REFLECTING THE INTERESTS OF

THE FOUNDER

OF THAMES AND HUDSON

THE DIRECTORS WISH TO EXPRESS

PARTICULAR GRATITUDE TO THE GOVERNORS AND

MASTER OF BIRKBECK COLLEGE,

UNIVERSITY OF LONDON,

FOR THEIR GRACIOUS SPONSORSHIP OF

THESE LECTURES

THE POLITICAL CAREER OF PETER PAUL RUBENS

C.V. WEDGWOOD

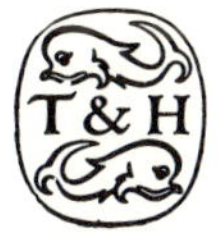

THAMES AND HUDSON
LONDON

When I was asked to contribute to the distinguished series of lectures in memory of Walter Neurath I felt both gratitude and pleasure. I am grateful to have been able to express in some small degree the admiration that all who are interested in the humanities must feel for the outstanding achievement of Walter Neurath. He perceived how a presentation which makes full and imaginative use of visual art can enrich the understanding of almost every branch of learning. The books that he inspired and produced have widened the visual appreciation of a whole generation and have illuminated the study of many subjects, among them my own field of history. It was also a great pleasure to me to express my gratitude by treating of one facet in the many-faceted career of Peter Paul Rubens, he too a man of wide, varied and constructive ideas, not least among them an interest in the production of good books nobly illustrated.

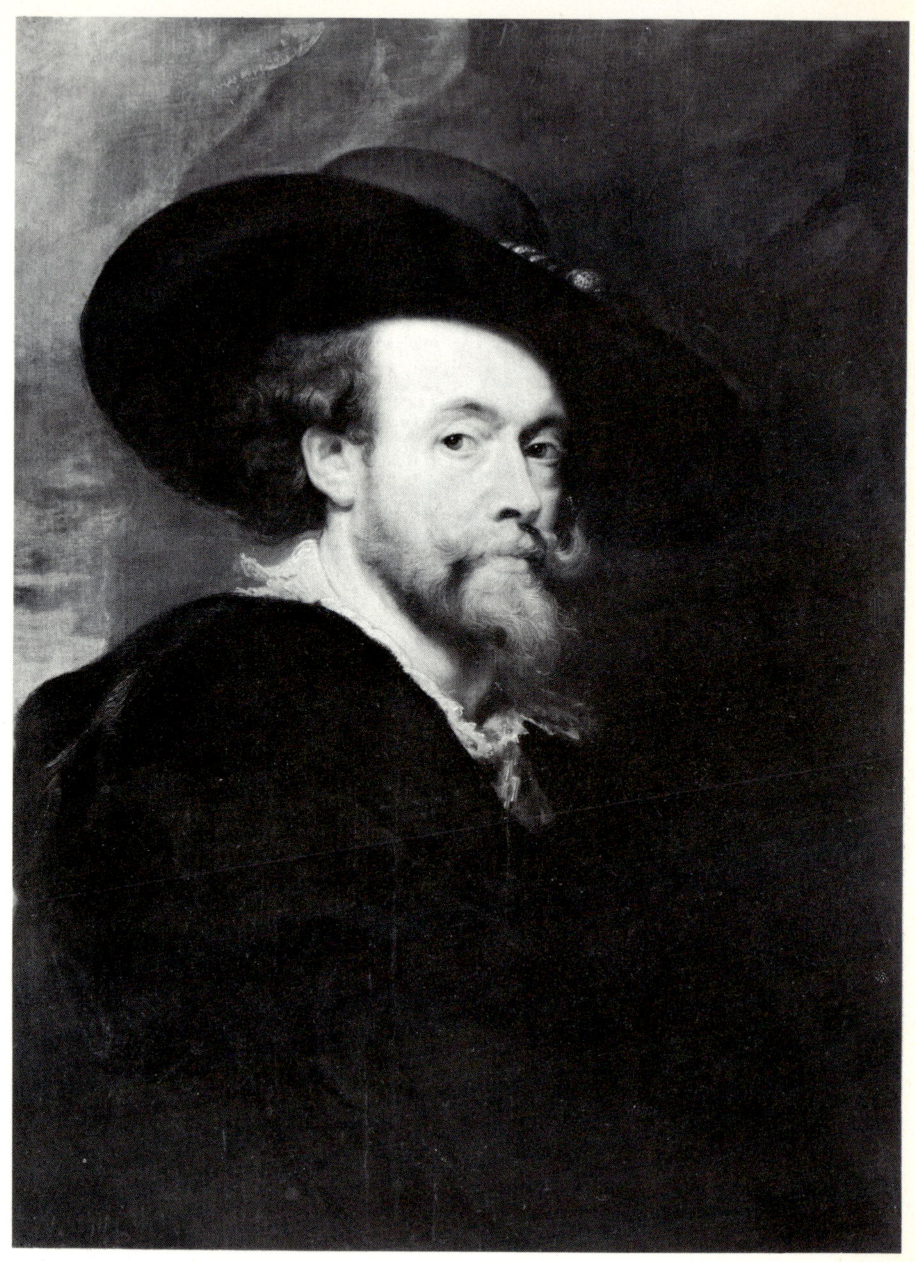

1 Rubens: Self-portrait

On 25 June 1629 King Charles I received Peter Paul Rubens in audience at Greenwich Palace. He received him not as ambassador of Spain but as an accredited envoy empowered to explore the possibilities of a peace with England. Rubens was not of high enough rank to fill the post of ambassador and he had been granted a patent of nobility to fit him for the lesser capacity in which he came. In effect he would do all the essential diplomatic work and a Spanish grandee would then be appointed to sign the treaty.

In the earlier seventeenth century when most rulers and leading statesmen collected works of art, either out of genuine interest, or as a status symbol, it had become a fairly common practice to use art-dealers, connoisseurs and occasionally artists themselves as unofficial contacts and sources of information. The collectors' world formed an international network not indeed at the highest level but at what may be described as an ancillary level of diplomacy.

Rubens, the most famous and successful painter in Europe, was also something of an expert in classical antiquities, a collector himself and an adviser of collectors. He had at one time sold his own fine collection of coins and cameos to the Duke of Buckingham, and he was in frequent contact with Sir Dudley Carleton, a famous connoisseur, who was English Ambassador at The Hague. He had executed a gigantic decorative commission for the Queen Mother of France, and on his visits to Paris on that occasion had sent useful reports to the princely rulers of the Spanish Netherlands to whom he was Court painter. He had also several times undertaken unofficial missions to Holland.

2 Gerard Honthorst: *Charles I*

3 Daniel Mytens: *Charles I and Henrietta Maria departing for the chase*

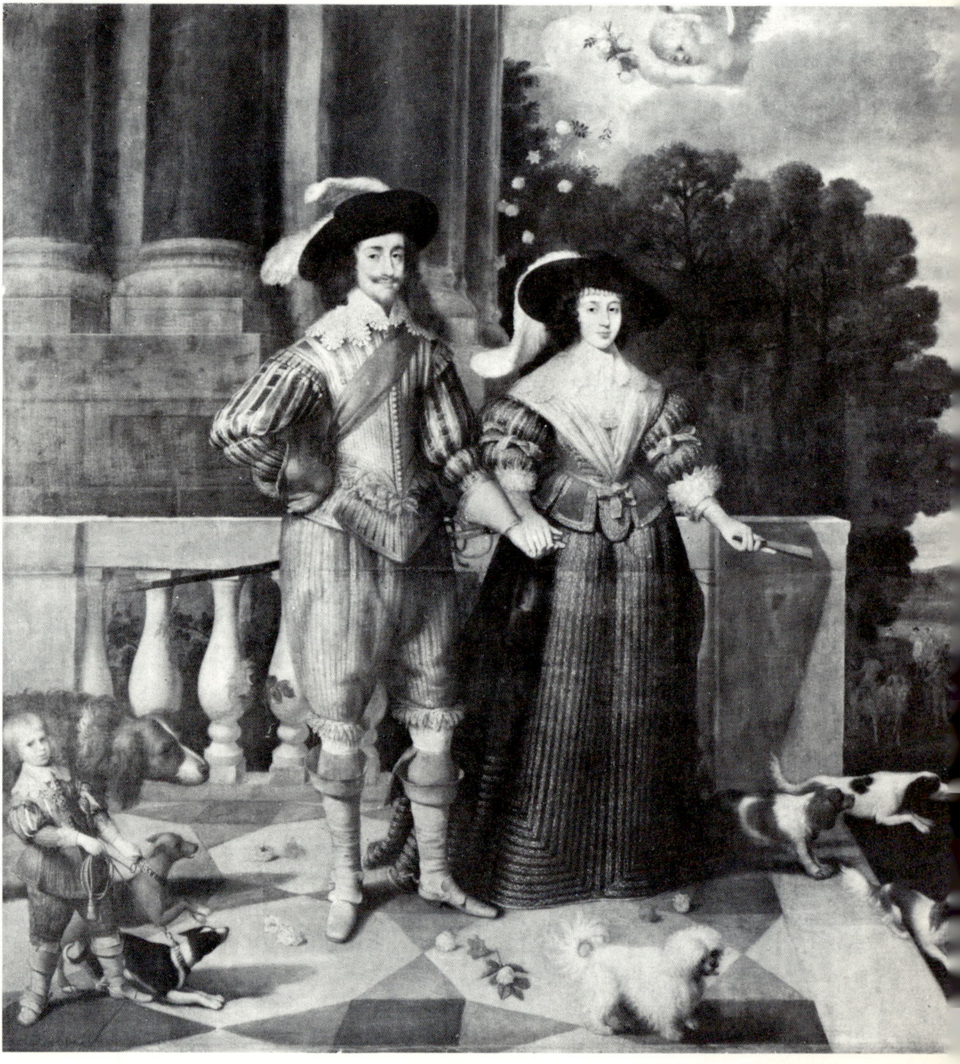

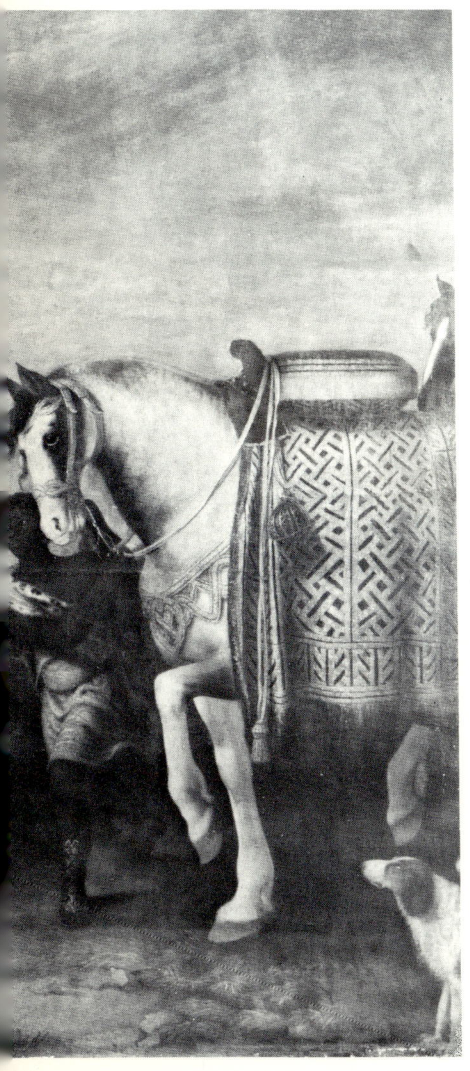

4 Rubens: *The Infanta Isabella with her patron saint, Elizabeth of Hungary*

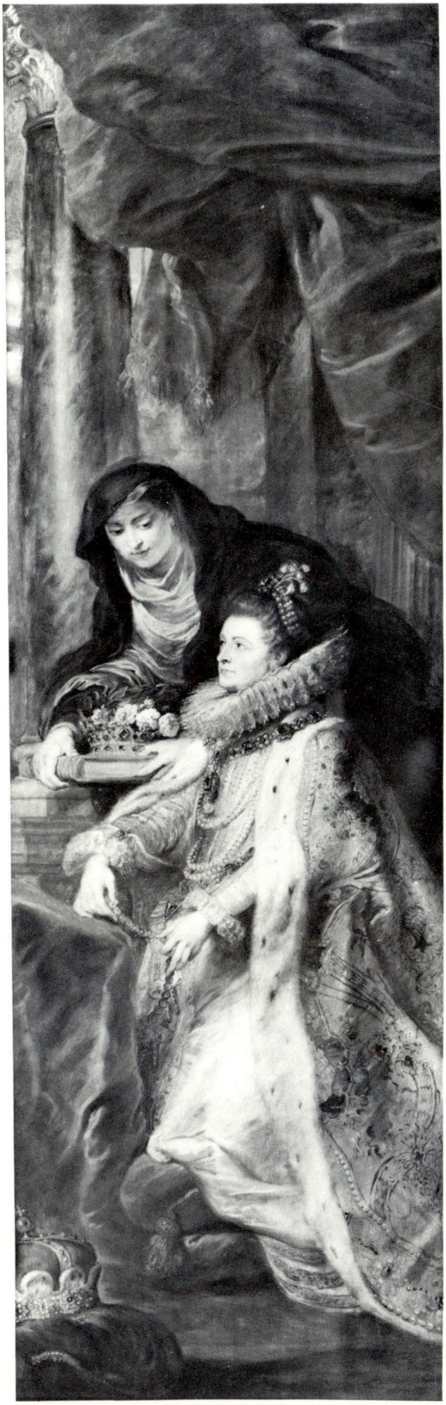

It was, none the less, unusual for so conventional a monarch as the King of Spain to use a bourgeois professional painter to negotiate a treaty with a fellow sovereign. The idea had of course come from the Infanta Isabella who governed the Netherlands and who had long experience of the social tact, political judgment and diplomatic skill of Rubens. She calculated rightly that, of all the royal patrons in Europe, Charles I would be the most receptive to such an envoy.

The question of protocol was solved by sending Rubens as the repre-sentative of the Infanta rather than the King, although he received his instructions from Madrid. Charles I was openly delighted and went so far as to command that a special message be sent with Rubens's pass-port indicating that 'His Majesty was well satisfied because he wishes to know a person of such merit.'

After the successful completion of his mission Rubens was knighted by the King. 'We grant him this title,' so ran the patent, 'because of his attachment to our person and the services he has rendered to us and to our subjects, his rare devotion to his own sovereign and the skill with which he has worked to restore a good understanding between the crowns of England and Spain.'

This was the zenith of Rubens's diplomatic career. But, after all, it is not as the architect of a minor treaty between England and Spain that he is chiefly remembered. My emphasis on his political skill may well suggest that I have got my priorities wrong.

This was a mistake that Rubens never made. In the course of an immensely productive, immensely successful and, on the whole, remarkably happy life, he persistently got his priorities right.

First and last, he was a painter. His other gifts and interests were all subsidiary to his *dolcissima professione* as he called it. Yet he had a multi-tude of other interests which, in a less well-organized man, would have diverted too much time from his painting. He was a distinguished amateur antiquary, in correspondence with half a dozen of the best scholars in Europe who recognized in him 'the most universal and remarkable knowledge'. He was eagerly interested, rather more amateurishly, in scientific invention. He compiled a treatise on colour for private circulation, which seems unfortunately to have vanished; he inquired into the then popular conundrum of perpetual motion; he was interested in fortifications and military architecture, indeed in architecture generally. He published a splendid book on the palaces of Genoa, intended as an example and guide to the architects of his beloved city of Antwerp. He was interested in natural history, and collected numberless pictures and accounts of unusual animals, some of which he brought into his pictures. He followed reports of maritime discoveries. In June 1628 he wrote with vibrating excitement, 'I have heard on good authority, but in secret and in great confidence, the positive report that they have discovered *ultra tropicum versus Austrum* a great country not to say a new world. This will be a memorable thing for our time. . . .'

5 Rubens: *Hippopotamus hunt*

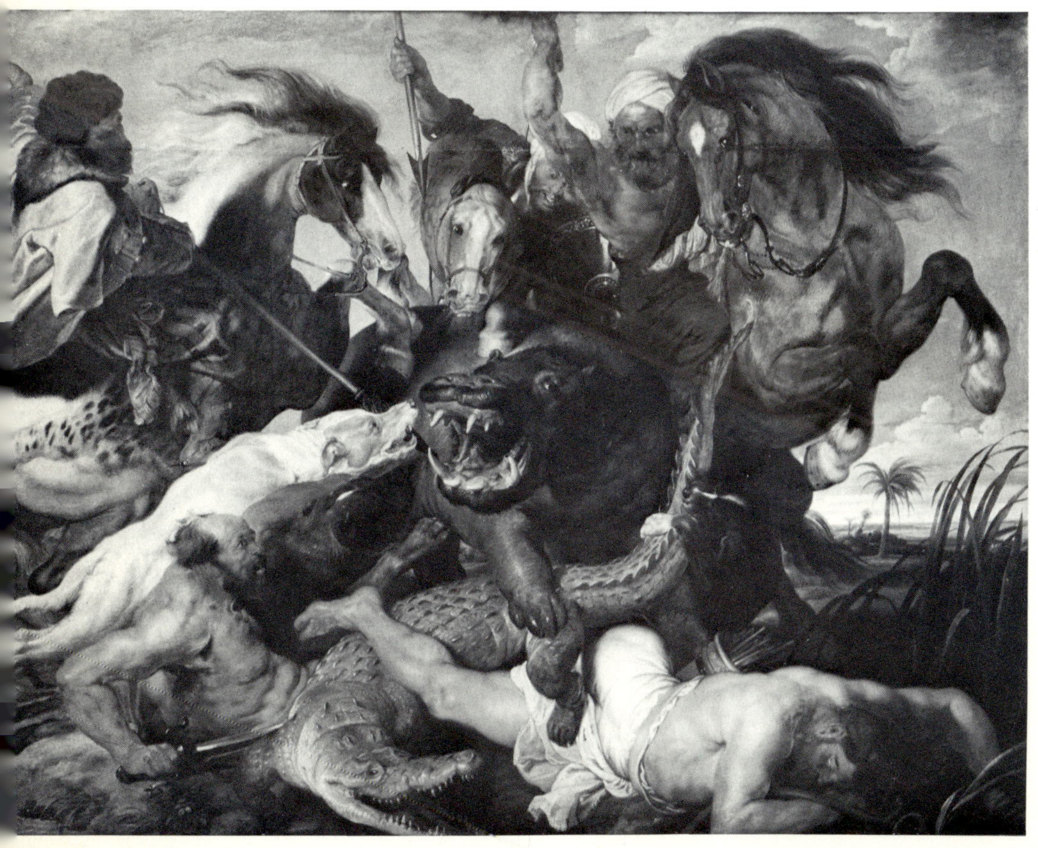

The discovery of Australia would indeed be memorable but was not to be completed until well over a century after the death of Rubens.

He was bilingual in Flemish and Italian, had serviceable French and Spanish and good Latin; he was keenly alive to contemporary thought and followed philosophic and religious speculations with critical interest (though he described Rosicrucianism as an *impostura*).

With all this, he had the social advantage of attractive manners and a ready flow of conversation. 'He is born to please and delight in all he does and says,' wrote his friend, the French naturalist and philosopher Claude Fabri de Peiresc. A young student painter, who accompanied him on a tour of the principal studios of Holland, described him as 'courteous and friendly to everyone, received with pleasure and beloved wherever he goes'. Admittedly he added, as an afterthought, that the great man had the reputation of being careful about money. There were reasons for that: money had not been plentiful in the otherwise happy home in which Rubens grew up. His widowed mother recorded with pride and gratitude in her will that her two youngest sons Philip and Peter Paul had supported themselves entirely from the age of fifteen.

All these interests and activities were encompassed within a sincere religious faith of a constructive and practical kind. He believed in hard work and the full use of his talents to gain an honest livelihood, for the glory of God and, within reason, for the assistance of the less fortunate. Some time ago it was fashionable to regard this attitude of mind as characteristic of Protestantism and an effect of the Reformation. But it was in fact just as common among Catholics.

A very clear example of Rubens's way of thinking occurs in a letter he wrote on the death of his friend Adam Elsheimer, whose singularly delicate and very small pictures he much admired, perhaps because his own genius lay in so different a direction. Elsheimer suffered from depression, from that breakdown of confidence which can so disastrously attack the creative artist – the lethargic despair which the Catholic Church then included under the sin of *accidie*: sloth.

When Elsheimer died Rubens wrote, 'I have never felt my heart more profoundly pierced by grief than at this news. . . . I pray God may

forgive his sin of sloth, by which he has deprived the world of the most
beautiful things . . . and finally reduced himself to despair, whereas with
his own hands he could have built up a great fortune and made himself
respected by all the world.' He then proceeded very sensibly to offer
help to the widow by arranging a good sale for her husband's surviving
pictures.

The span of Rubens's life – he was born in 1577 and died in 1640 –
covers the latter end of the Counter-Reformation, an epoch in which
religious wars, which were always half political and often wholly so,
repeatedly involved most of western Europe. The revolt of the Netherlands against Spain began ten years before he was born and ended eight
years after his death. As a citizen of Antwerp, which was ruined by the
division of the Netherlands, he was directly concerned. The prolonged
power struggle in central Europe, the Thirty Years War, covered the
latter part of his life and figures prominently in his correspondence. So
do the Huguenot revolts in France.

As a loyal subject of the Spanish Netherlands and a devout Catholic,
his politics were indivisible from his religion. But he was deeply concerned for the welfare of his country and its people, and for at least

6 Adam Elsheimer: *St Paul on Malta*

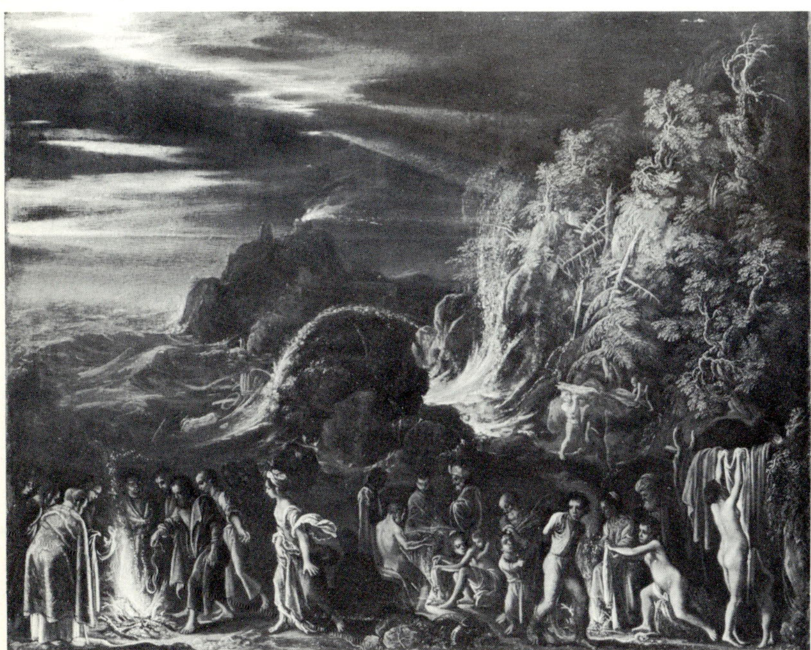

fifteen years of his life he was active in minor, and finally in major, diplomatic activity tending to one end only: peace with the Dutch and the harmonious reunion of the Netherlands.

The politics of the Netherlands conditioned his life from the outset. In 1567 when Protestant rioting in Antwerp heralded the revolt against Philip II, Rubens's father, a distinguished lawyer with Calvinist sympathies, fled with his wife and family to Cologne. Here he was appointed secretary to Anna of Saxony, wife of the Prince of Orange, who was beginning to organize the resistance to Spain. Anna, passionate, unbalanced and demanding, made him her lover. The affair was discovered, the Princess divorced and Jan Rubens imprisoned. His wife loyally stood by him and was largely instrumental in securing his pardon. In the meantime she supported their family of four by taking in lodgers. Two more children were born after they were reunited, Philip in 1574 and Peter Paul in 1577.

In spite of exile and poverty, it was a happy home. Years later Rubens was to write with gratitude of his 'great affection for the city of Cologne where I lived for the first ten years of my life'. His mother was evidently a good wife, a good mother and a good manager. His father, a man of learning who had seen something of the world, started his younger sons in their classical studies and taught them to speak fluent Italian. From the first the two brothers were deeply attached to one another.

When Rubens was ten his father died and his mother, who had a small property in Antwerp, returned to the Netherlands and, as a matter of course, to the Catholic faith. Rubens was to be a sincerely practising Catholic for the rest of his life, though he retained a certain sympathetic insight into the Reformed religion. His elder brother, Philip, a natural scholar, became one of the best pupils of the famous professor of Louvain, Justus Lipsius, the editor of Tacitus and Seneca, who taught a Christianized Stoicism as a guide to moral conduct: an attitude of mind which Rubens also cultivated.

As Peter Paul was quick, industrious and sociable his mother got him a post in a noble household, but he stayed only for a year and then persuaded her to let him embark on the more uncertain career of a

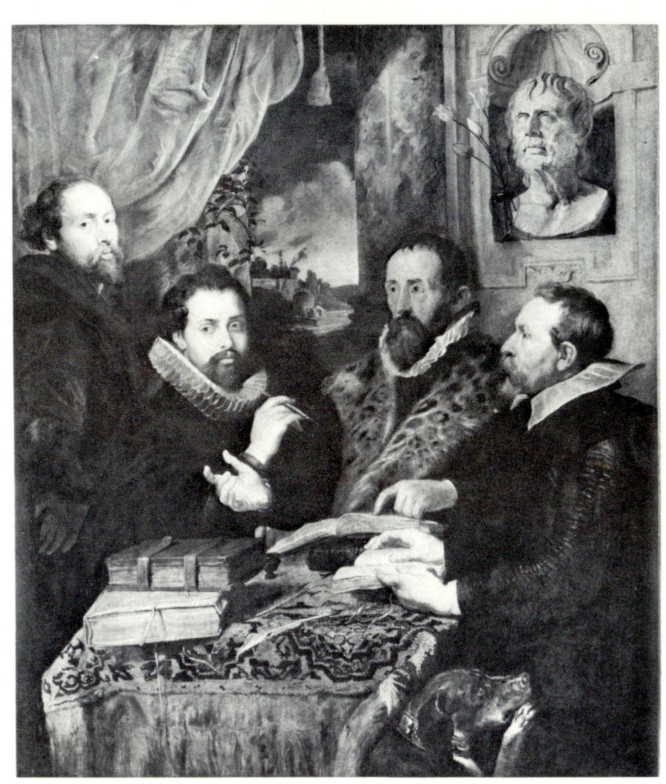

7 Rubens: *Justus Lipsius with his pupils*

painter. At the age of twenty-three, having learnt all that the studios of Antwerp had to teach, he set out in May 1600 to work and study in Italy.

Painting, and not the politics of his homeland, was at this time uppermost in his heart and mind, for no politically minded young Fleming would have chosen to leave his country in the year 1600.

The revolt of the Netherlands against Spain had reached deadlock. The North, the United Provinces with Holland at their head, had become independent and largely Calvinist. Paradoxically the South (where the revolt had first begun) had become increasingly loyalist and Catholic. The growing maritime and commercial strength of the United Provinces threatened the overseas power of Spain and undermined the prosperity of the South by blockading the Scheldt. The King

15

of Spain could not afford to renounce his right over the North and it was equally in the interests of the loyalist South to support the Spanish war as victory alone would end the blockade and the economic competition which was ruining them.

Just before his death, Philip II raised the morale of the loyalists by according nominal independence to the South. He appointed his son-in-law, the Austrian Archduke Albert, to rule over the Netherlands independently of the Spanish Crown – an independence which would be continued if, as was hoped, his wife the Infanta Isabella had children. The Netherlands would thus remain linked into the great combine of Spanish-Austrian alliances but would have independent status in all but foreign policy.

The arrival of the Infanta and her husband in Brussels in 1600 was greeted by an outburst of hopeful rejoicing. A new era seemed to be opening for the war-wearied Netherlands. But by this time the young Rubens was on his way to Italy. He stayed in Italy for eight years working for the Duke of Mantua, a lavish patron of the arts, who employed him to make designs for Court masques and entertainments, and to copy the works of the great masters for the Duke's collection and sometimes to advise him about purchases. Allowed a great deal of freedom, he spent long periods in Rome studying, sketching and diligently perfecting his technical skill.

In 1603 he had his first experience of what may almost be called diplomacy. The Duke of Mantua needed to stand well with the King of Spain whose influence was paramount in Italy. On the occasion of the marriage of Philip III, he therefore prepared superb presents for the King, the Queen and their chief minister the Duke of Lerma: an elegant coach, six beautifully matched bay horses, gold, silver and crystal vases, and sixteen copies (not by Rubens) of works by Raphael, Titian and other great masters.

Rubens, as the most competent of his servants, was charged to convey all these in safety to the Spanish Court. His letters, written to the Duke's steward, give a vivid impression of his resourcefulness during a long and hazardous journey. The crystal vases, the coach and all six horses, groomed with wine (*bagni di vino*), arrived in splendid condition at Valladolid. Not so the pictures: twenty-six days of continuous rain, 'a thing most unusual in Spain', penetrated the wooden chest, double oil-cloth and tin casing in which they had been packed under Rubens's personal supervision. Only momentarily at a loss, he immediately set to work to repair the damage so that the Duke of Lerma, on receiving them, suspected nothing – and apparently assumed that they were originals. Rubens was too tactful to undeceive him.

Lerma is an undistinguished figure in Spanish history, but he must be given credit for at least one gesture of intelligent patronage: he commissioned the unknown young Fleming with the courtly manners to paint his portrait. The result was the great equestrian portrait now in the Prado. Boldly, Rubens attempted the difficult feat of painting the Duke riding straight towards the spectator. In his masterly design the splendid curve of the horse's neck and head lead the eye upwards to the head of the rider with firm and majestic effect.

Rubens remained in the Duke of Mantua's service for another five years, but in the autumn of 1608 he was recalled to Antwerp by news of his mother's illness. He travelled fast, but she died before he reached home. It had been his intention to return to Italy where his reputation was established and growing. But events in the Netherlands caused him to change his mind. The Archduke offered him a post as one of the Court painters. As an encouragement to the still thriving school of painters in the Southern Netherlands, the Archduke and his wife had several painters permanently attached to their Court. More important than this offer was the perseverance of the Archduke in overtures to the Dutch which culminated in the establishment of a truce to run for twelve years, a period during which it was hoped the conditions of a lasting peace might be agreed. This hopeful move, possibly more than anything else, decided Rubens to stay in the Netherlands. On 10 April 1609 he wrote to a friend in Rome: 'I have not yet made up my mind whether to remain in my country or to return forever to Rome. . . . The Archduke and the Most Serene Infanta have had letters written urging me to remain. . . . Their offers are very generous but I have little desire

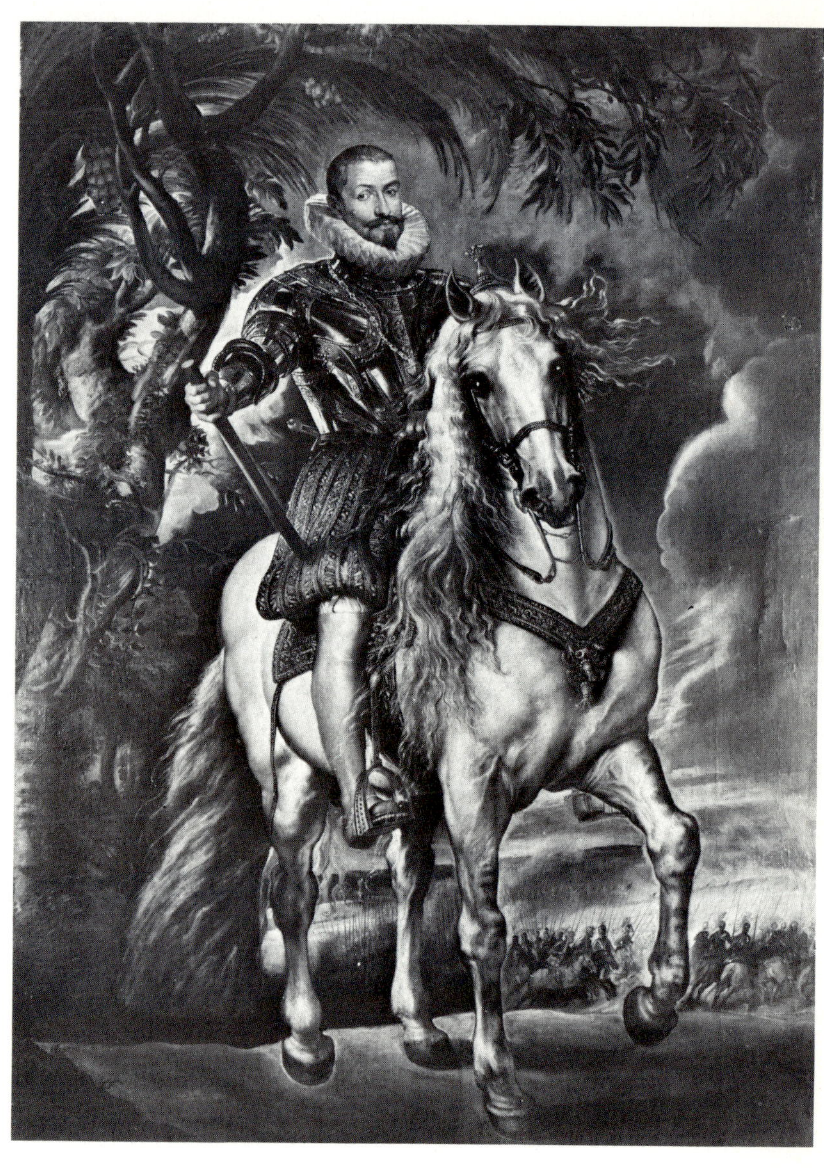

8 Rubens: *Equestrian portrait of the Duke of Lerma*

to become a courtier again. . . . The peace, or rather the truce, for many years will without doubt be ratified, and during this period it is believed that our country will flourish again.'

The truce was ratified four days later. Everything now conspired to make Rubens stay in the Netherlands. His brother Philip, previously a frequent visitor to Italy, had married and settled down to a responsible position in the city administration of Antwerp. In September 1609 Rubens was duly appointed a Court painter with special permission to reside in Antwerp (most Court painters had to live in Brussels). Ten days later he married Isabella Brant, a bride who had evidently been found for him by his brother and sister-in-law, for she was the

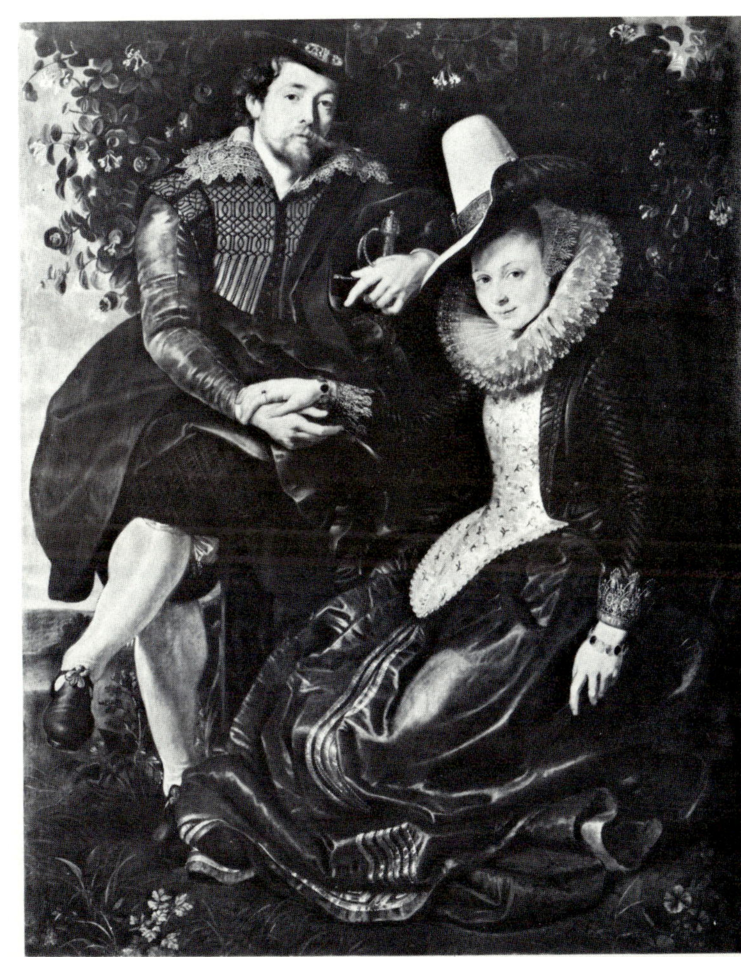

9 Rubens: *The artist with his first wife, Isabella Brant*

niece of Philip's wife. It proved a singularly happy marriage, and
Rubens celebrated the occasion by painting a gay and elegant wedding
portrait, a picture in which the clear colours and precise treatment of
detail recall the characteristics of the Flemish school during the Golden
Age of the fifteenth century. From now on Rubens was fully committed
to his own country.

Peace for many years was assured and the hope, which Rubens
shared with most of his compatriots, that 'our country will flourish
again' seemed to be realized. Trade revived as the Scheldt was freed

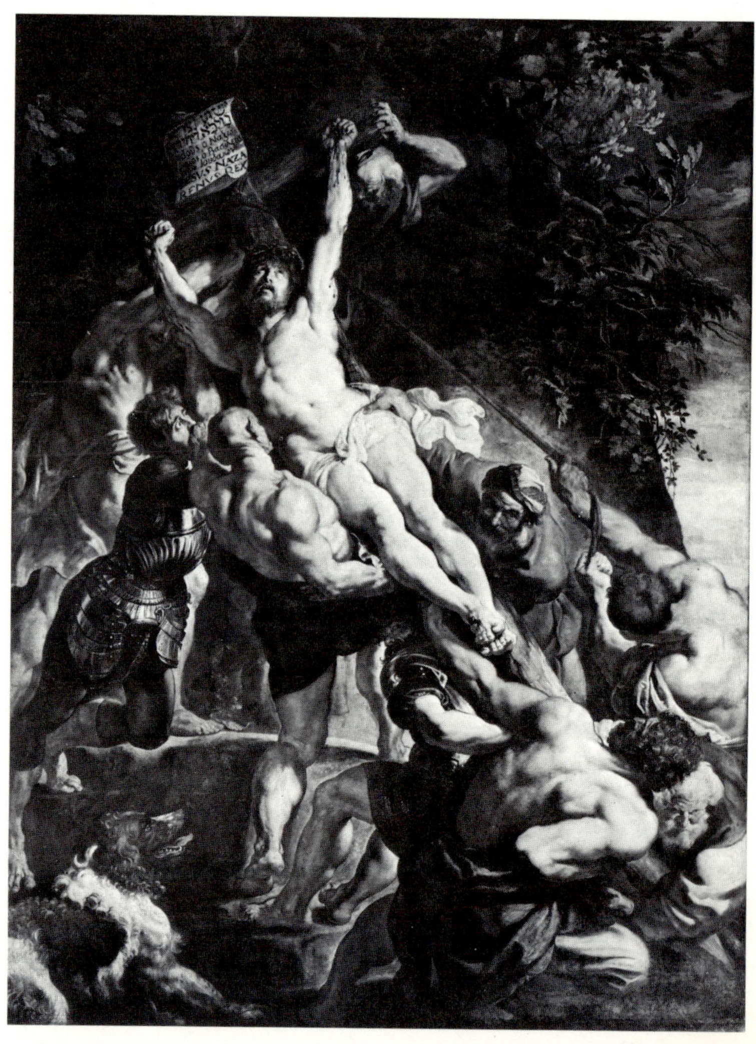

from blockade, and with returning prosperity came revival in hope and revival in all the arts of peace. Rubens was in demand at once to paint altarpieces for the beautification of churches neglected during the hard times of the long war, but now thankfully restored.

In these years of truce he painted the powerful *Elevation of the Cross* and the deeply moving *Descent from the Cross*, both now in Antwerp Cathedral, and several versions of the *Adoration of the Magi*. Of these the most exciting in colour and rhythm is perhaps the one now in the Antwerp Museum, with a typical Rubens tribute to the universality of

10 Rubens: *Elevation of the Cross*

11 Rubens: *Descent from the Cross*

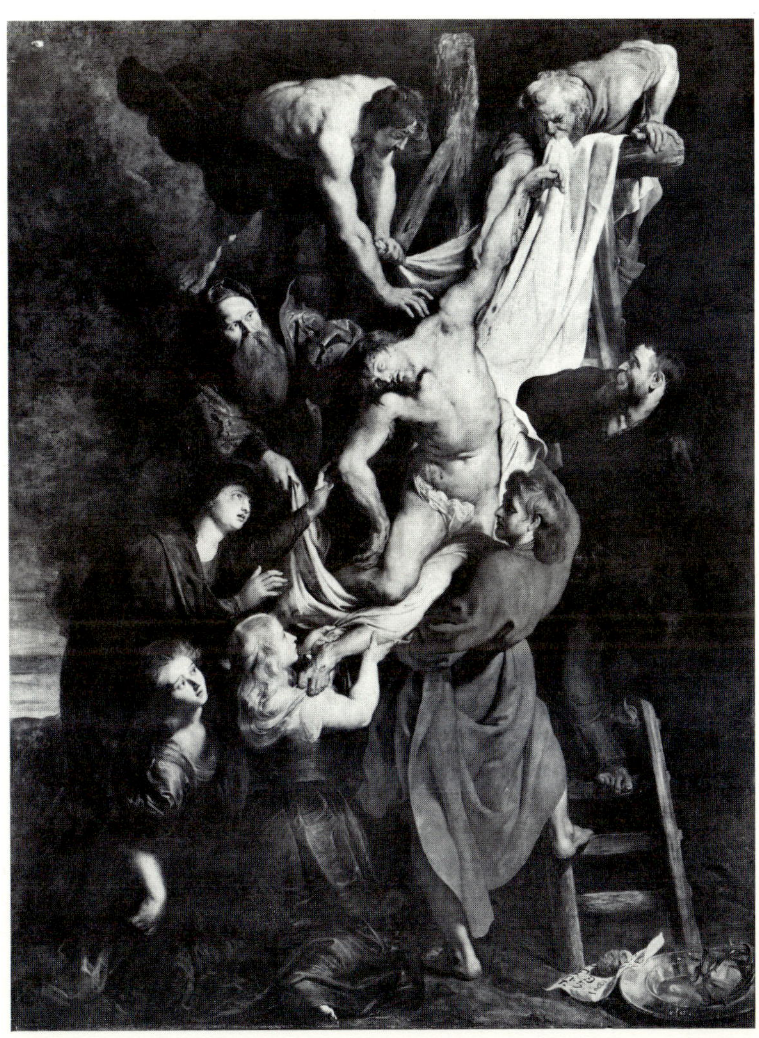

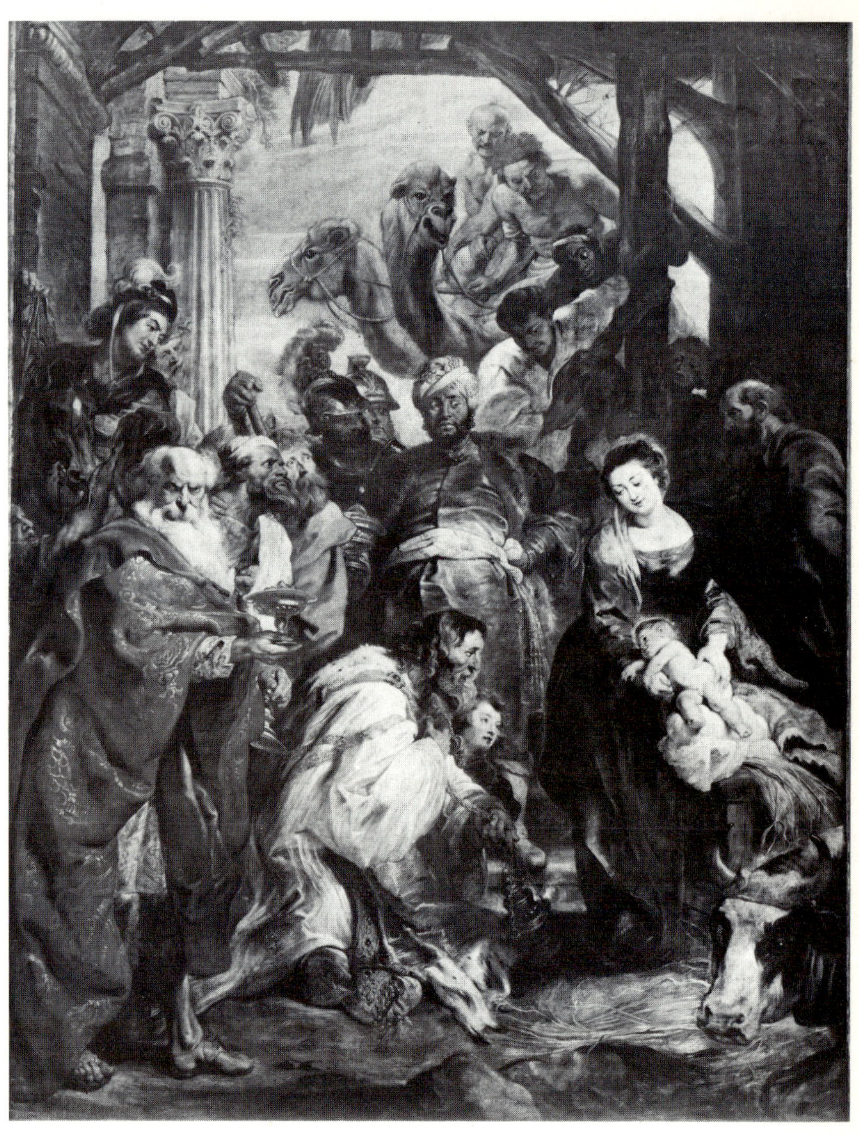

12 Rubens: *Adoration of the Magi*

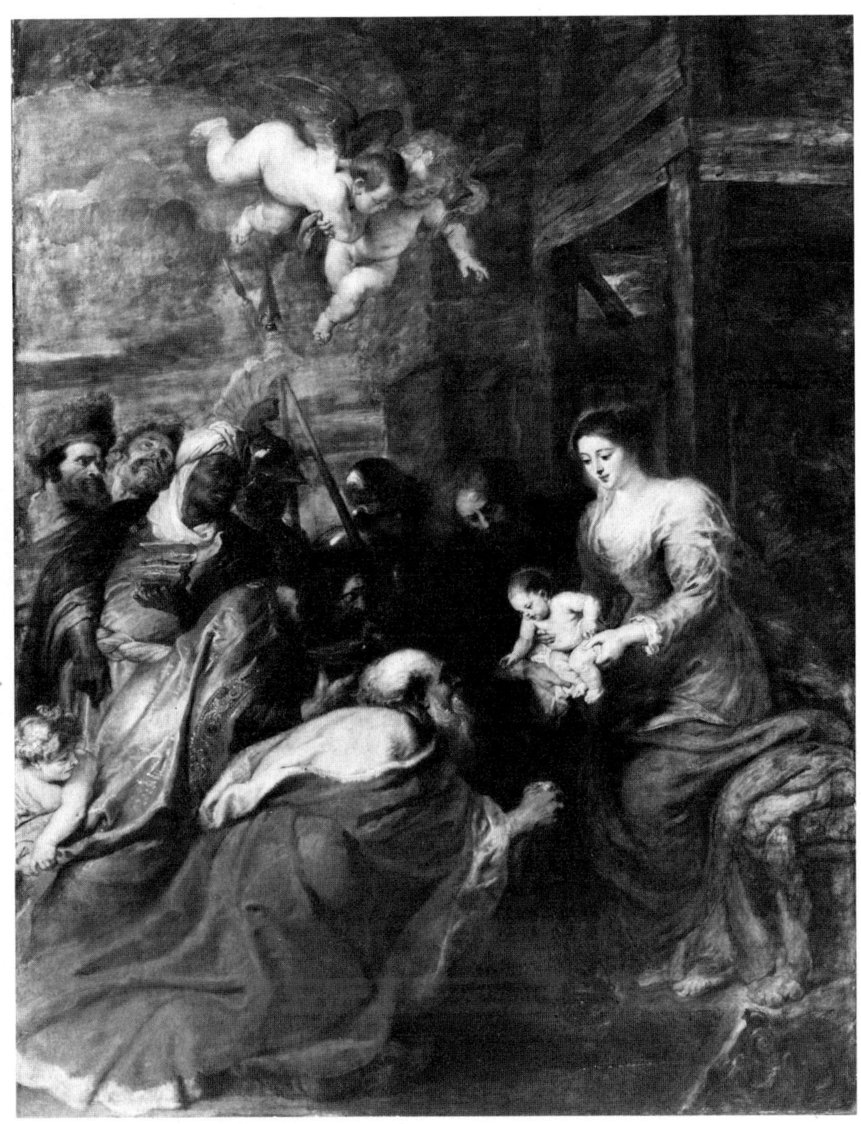

13 Rubens: *Adoration of the Magi*

the Faith in the Eastern figures and tall camels appearing at the back. The most poetic version is surely that which now hangs in King's College Chapel, Cambridge. Smaller pictures, like the Madonnas surrounded by garlands of fruit and flowers in which he collaborated with his older contemporary and friend Jan Brueghel, or the delightful *Holy Family with St John and St Elizabeth*, strike a more domestic note. His Madonnas of this period usually bear an idealized resemblance to his wife, and in the Holy Family the children are recognizably his two sons.

14 Rubens: *Adoration of the Magi*

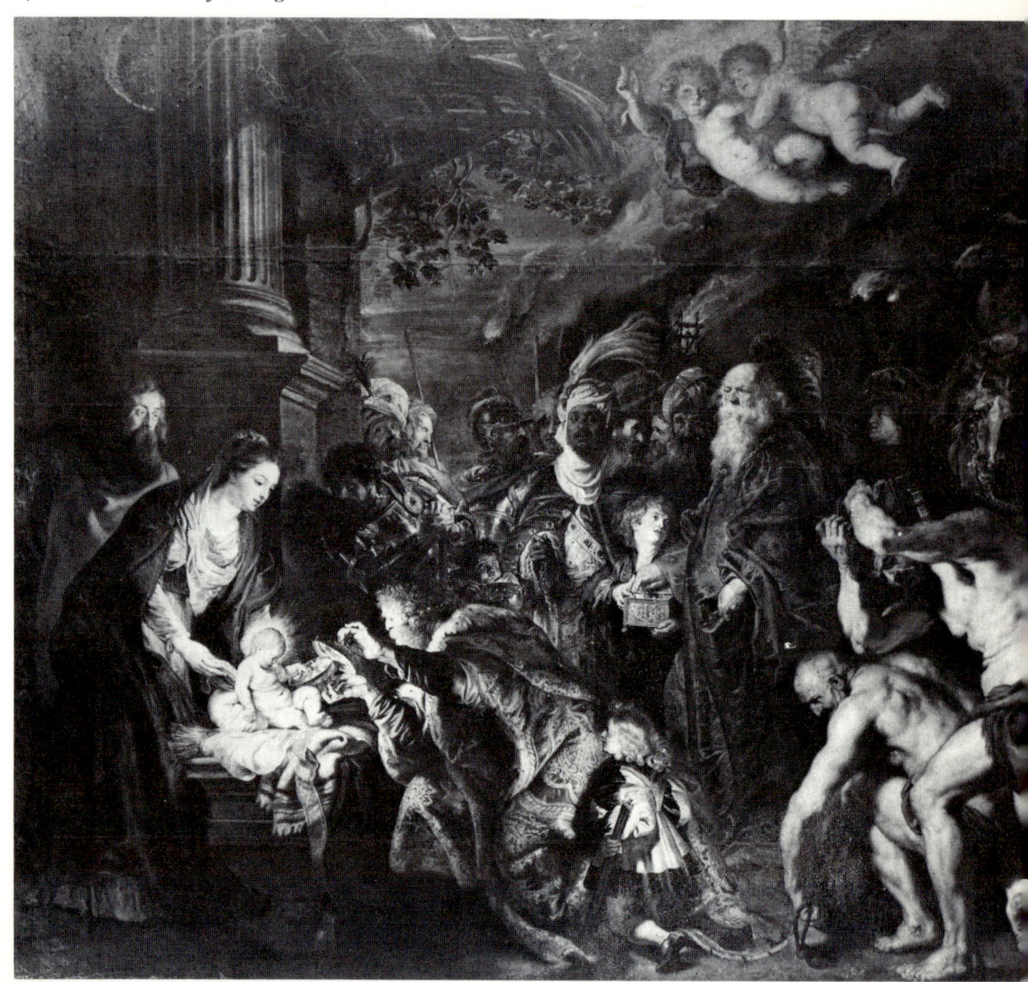

Apart from his innumerable commissions, secular as well as religious, he found time to make drawings to illustrate devotional works issued during this decade by the famous Plantin Press, the official printer to the Catholic Church. Christophe Plantin's grandson and successor, Balthasar Moretus, had formed a lifelong friendship with Rubens when both were schoolboys. They lived near to each other in Antwerp and Rubens provided the illustrations at a cheap rate because he could draw them at any time of day when he had ten minutes to spare, or when the light was not good enough for painting.

15 Rubens: *Holy Family with St John and St Elizabeth*

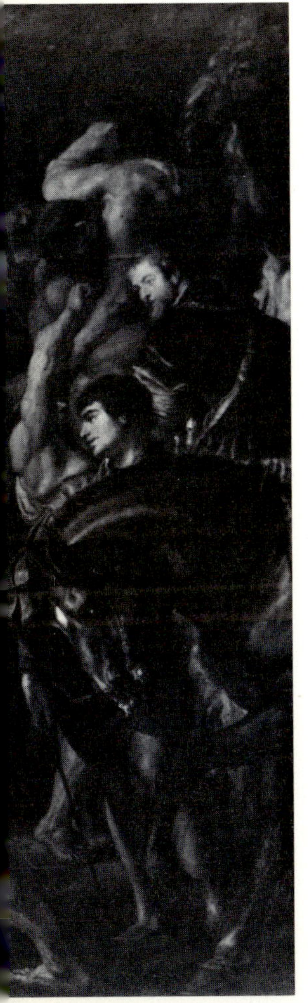

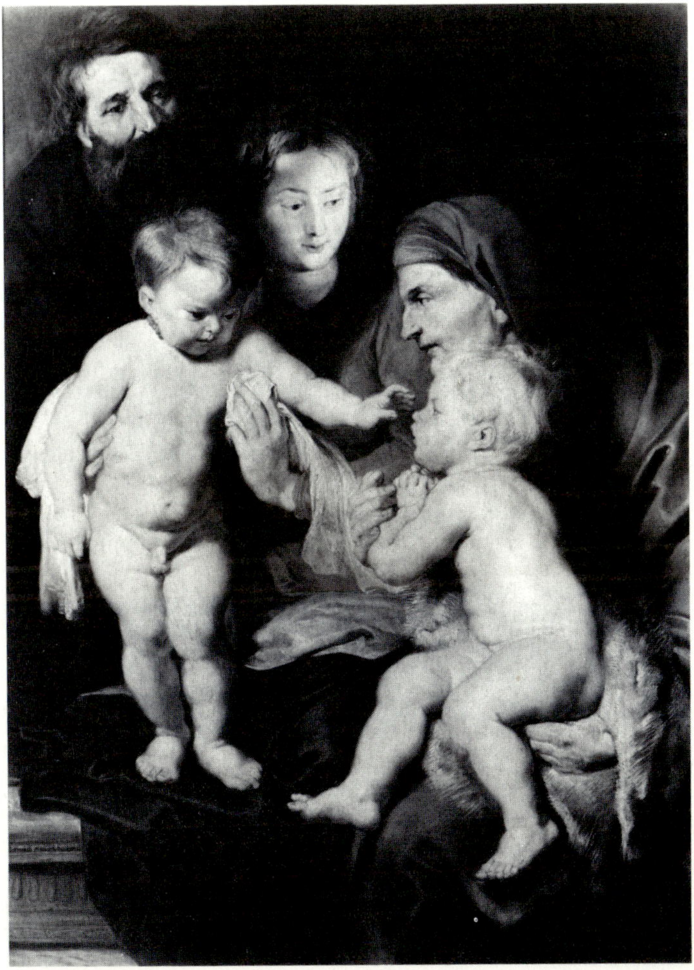

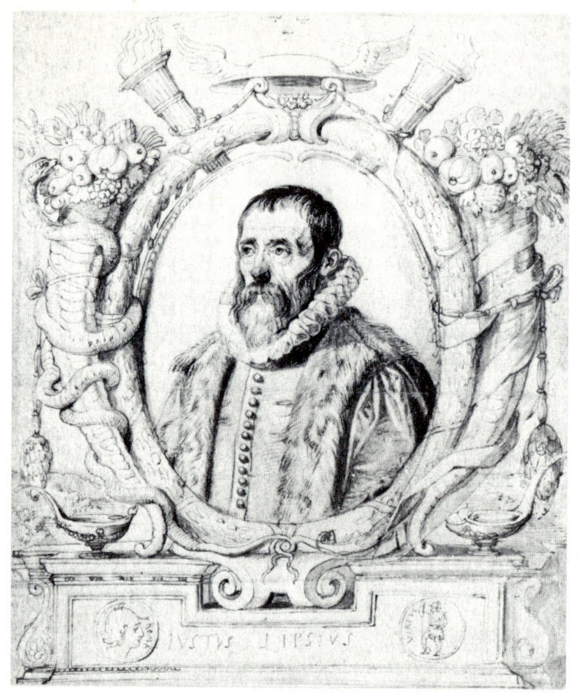

16 Rubens: Design for title-page of Justus Lipsius's edition of the works of Seneca

17 Rubens: Second design for the printer's mark of the Plantin Press made for Balthasar Moretus

18 Title-page of *Jacobi Bosii Crux Triumphans*, engraved by Galle after Rubens

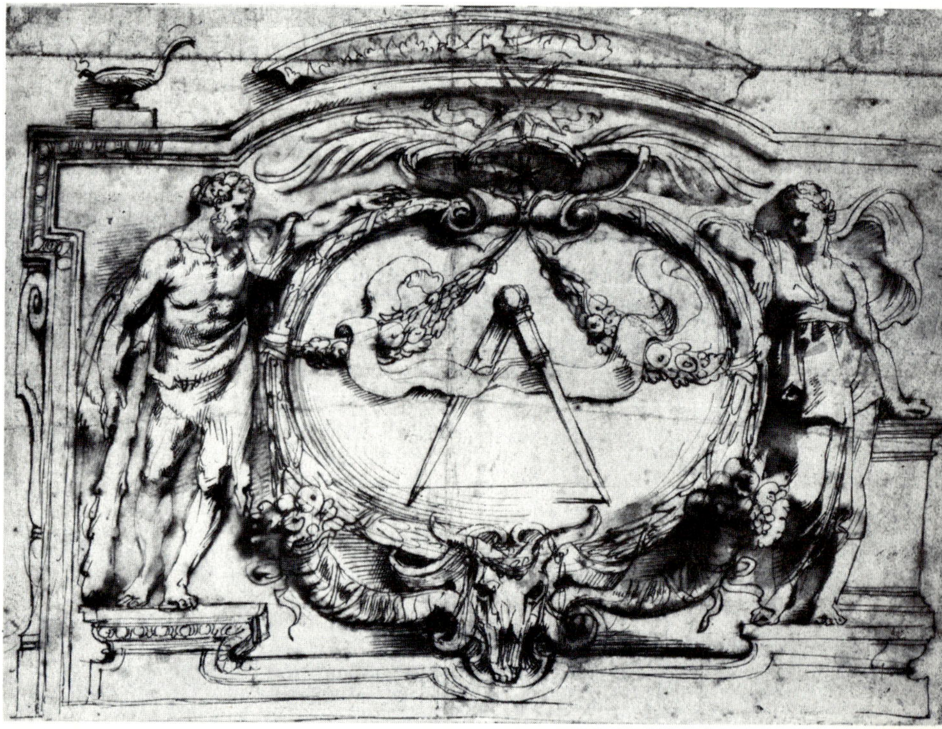

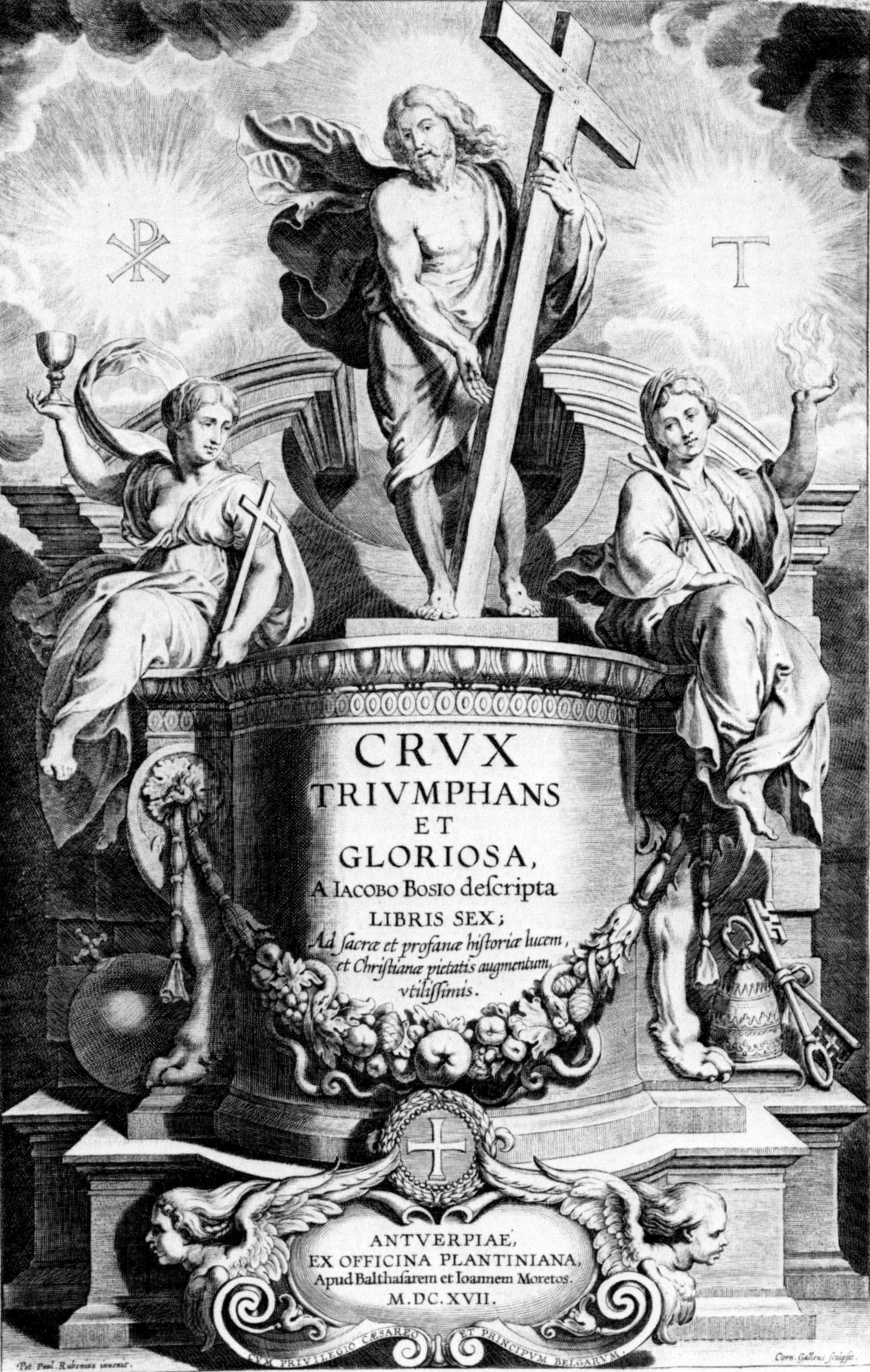
CRVX
TRIVMPHANS
ET
GLORIOSA,
A Iacobo Bosio descripta
LIBRIS SEX;
Ad sacræ et profanæ historiæ lucem,
et Christianæ pietatis augmentum,
vtilissimis.
ANTVERPIAE,
EX OFFICINA PLANTINIANA,
Apud Balthasarem et Ioannem Moretos.
M.DC.XVII.
CVM PRIVILEGIO CÆSAREO ET PRINCIPVM BELGARVM.
Pet. Paul. Rubenius inuenit.
Corn. Galleus sculpsit.

His nephew Philip, whom he adopted into his family after the early death of Philip's father, left an account of how Rubens organized his working day. He was up by four and heard Mass before breakfast; then worked until about five in the afternoon, receiving visitors while he worked or, if there were no visitors, dictating letters or listening to readings from his favourite authors. In the late afternoon, after dinner, he went out walking or riding, or entertained his friends.

His religion was both a conviction and an inspiration. Although his active extrovert temperament fitted him better for the celebration of physical beauty and the splendour of creation than for the interpretation of the inner life, he brought great tragic feeling to his Crucifixions and Martyrdoms and, in one picture – the *Last Communion of St Francis of Assisi* – he marvellously expressed in the wasted features of the saint the consummation of mystical union in the moment of death.

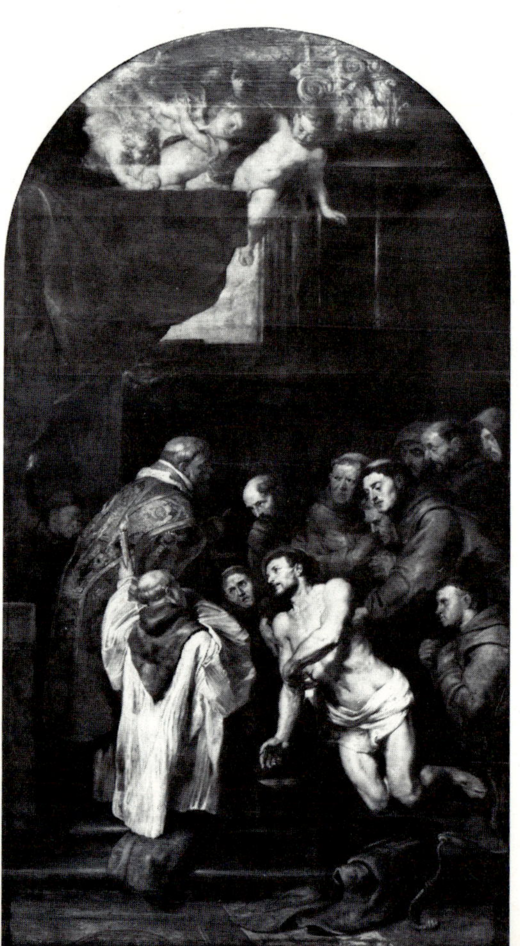

19 Rubens: *Last Communion of St Francis of Assisi*

Meanwhile the eleven-year truce was running out and negotiations for a permanent peace came to nothing. In April 1621 the divided Netherlands were again at war. A few weeks later Archduke Albert died. He had no heir but the widowed Infanta Isabella was immediately appointed Governor by the King of Spain and continued to exercise almost independent power.

In the renewed war with the Dutch the position of the Spanish Netherlands was far more favourable than it had been before the truce. There had been economic recovery and the strength and morale of the Army had been built up by the great Genoese General, Ambrogio Spinola. Just before the truce expired Spinola had profited by the disturbances in Germany, which heralded the Thirty Years War, to occupy a part of the Rhineland, a move which presented a serious threat to the Dutch land frontiers. The Dutch countered by blockading the Scheldt as soon as the truce expired.

Rubens was in touch with Sir Dudley Carleton, English Ambassador at The Hague, a great collector and connoisseur. Through this useful contact he took some part in the confidential but abortive negotiations with the Dutch which preceded the resumption of hostilities. In the following autumn, when he was commissioned by Marie de Médicis, Queen Mother of France, to decorate her new Luxembourg Palace, the Infanta saw an opportunity of again using his diplomatic talents. When he went to Paris to lay his designs before Marie de Médicis, he was entrusted with presents and compliments to her from the Infanta, and privately charged to notice and report on conditions at the French Court. This was no mere frivolous interest: the rivalry between France and Spain had been the dominant factor in European politics for over a century. During the Regency of Marie de Médicis for her young son, this policy had been reversed and the monarchies of France and Spain had been bound together by a double marriage alliance. The vital question, when Rubens journeyed to Paris early in 1622, was whether these dynastic marriages would be a sufficient bond to prevent the King from repudiating his mother's foreign policy now that he was of age and had already excluded her from power.

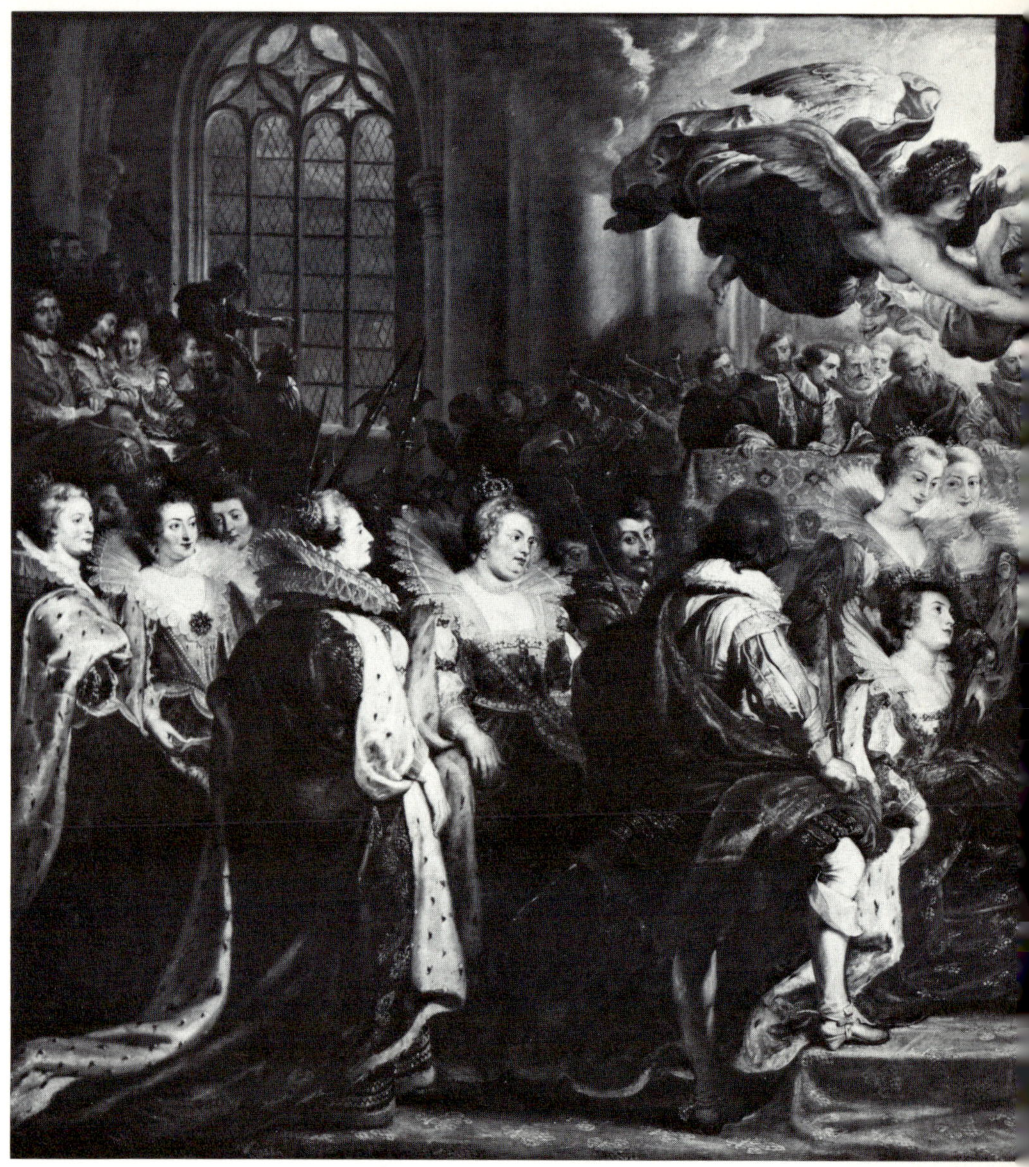

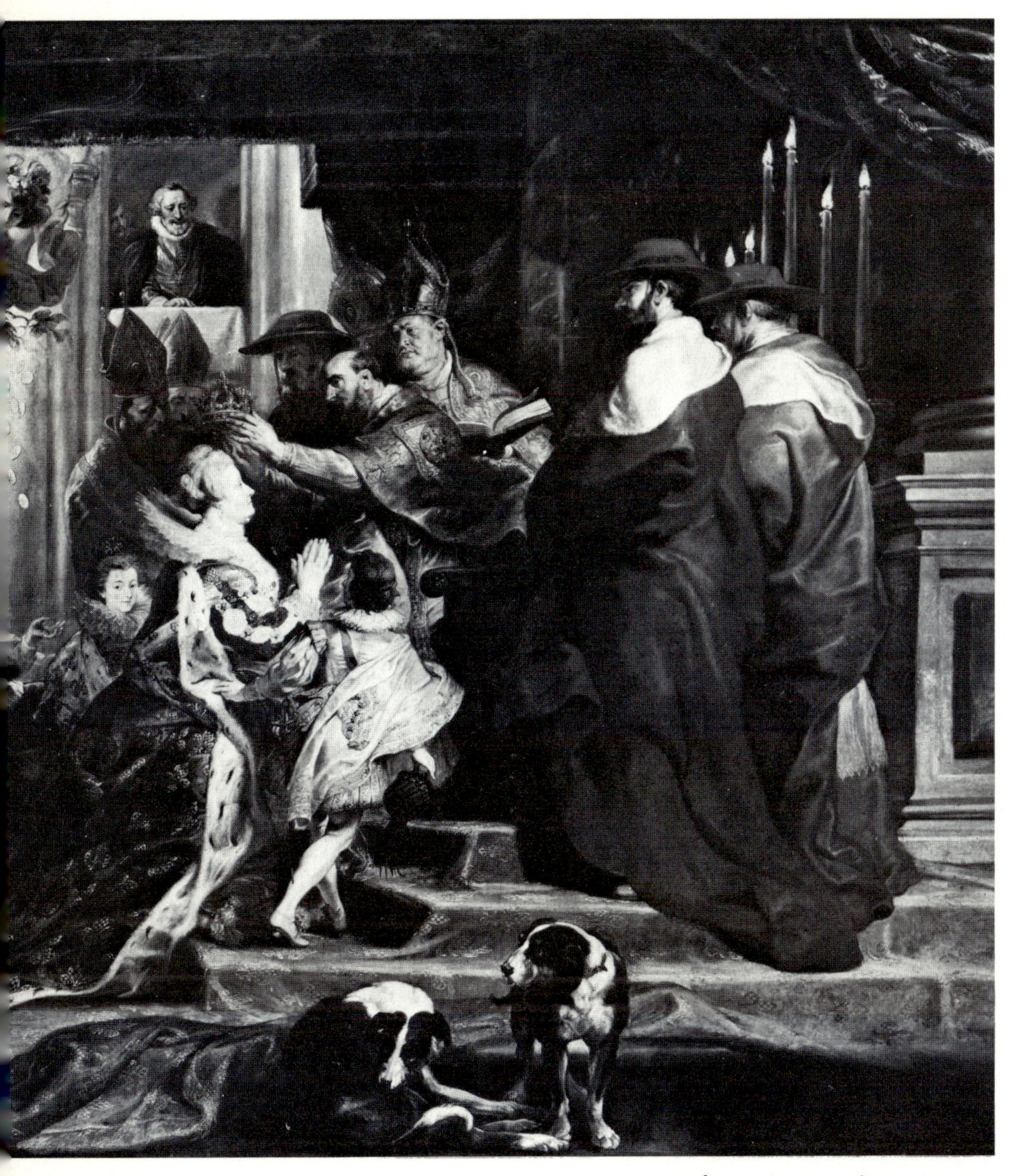

20 Rubens: *Coronation of Marie de Médicis*

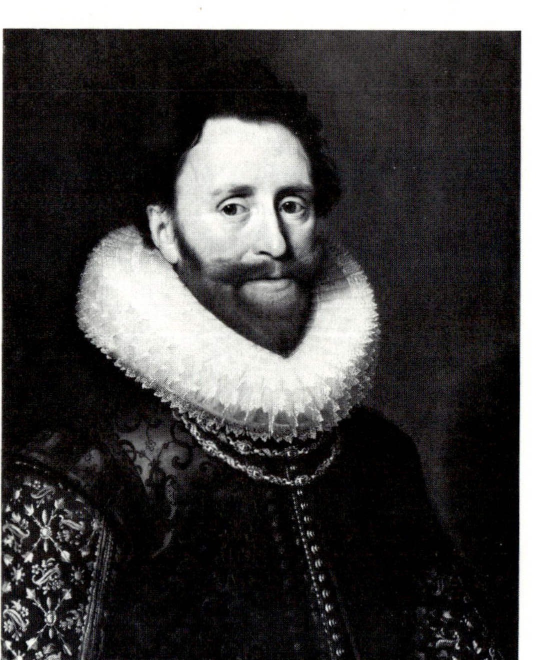

21 Part of a letter from Rubens to Sir Dudley Carleton dated 26 May 1618

22 Michiel van Miereveldt: *Sir Dudley Carleton*

23 Philippe de Champaigne: *Triple portrait of Cardinal Richelieu*

Rubens came back from his first visit with reasonable confidence that the Franco-Spanish alliance would hold. But when he returned, with the completed pictures, three years later the situation had deteriorated. The formidable Cardinal Richelieu was now the King's chief minister and had already made strategic moves against Spain in the Val Telline, while advocating the marriage of the King's sister Henrietta Maria to Charles I, who was at war with Spain. Richelieu commissioned a picture from Rubens – by 1625 it was a status symbol to own a Rubens – but he discouraged any further visits to Paris by holding up payment for the pictures so far completed and surreptitiously advising against his employment for a projected second series of pictures to celebrate the career of Henri IV.

But Richelieu could not prevent Rubens from meeting the Duke of Buckingham, the influential favourite of Charles I who had come over for the wedding of the Princess. Buckingham sat for his portrait, listened to Rubens's flattering hints of the great part he might play as a peacemaker and agreed to keep in private touch with him through the intermediary of Balthasar Gerbier, a minor artist, by origin a Zeelander, who had charge of the Duke's foreign correspondence.

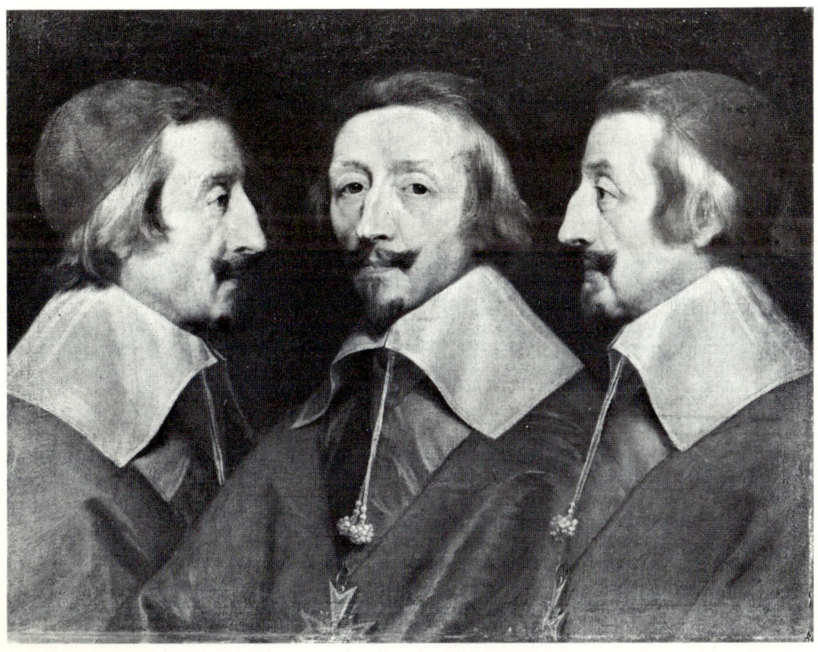

This hopeful contact was brought to nothing, not by the machinations of Richelieu but by the folly of Buckingham, who in a vain pursuit of naval glory soon afterwards involved England in a war with France in addition to the existing war with Spain. 'When I consider the caprice and arrogance of Buckingham,' wrote Rubens, 'I pity that young King who, through false counsel, is needlessly throwing himself and his kingdom into such an extremity. For anyone can start a war . . . but he cannot so easily end it.'

24 Rubens: *Equestrian portrait of the Duke of Buckingham*

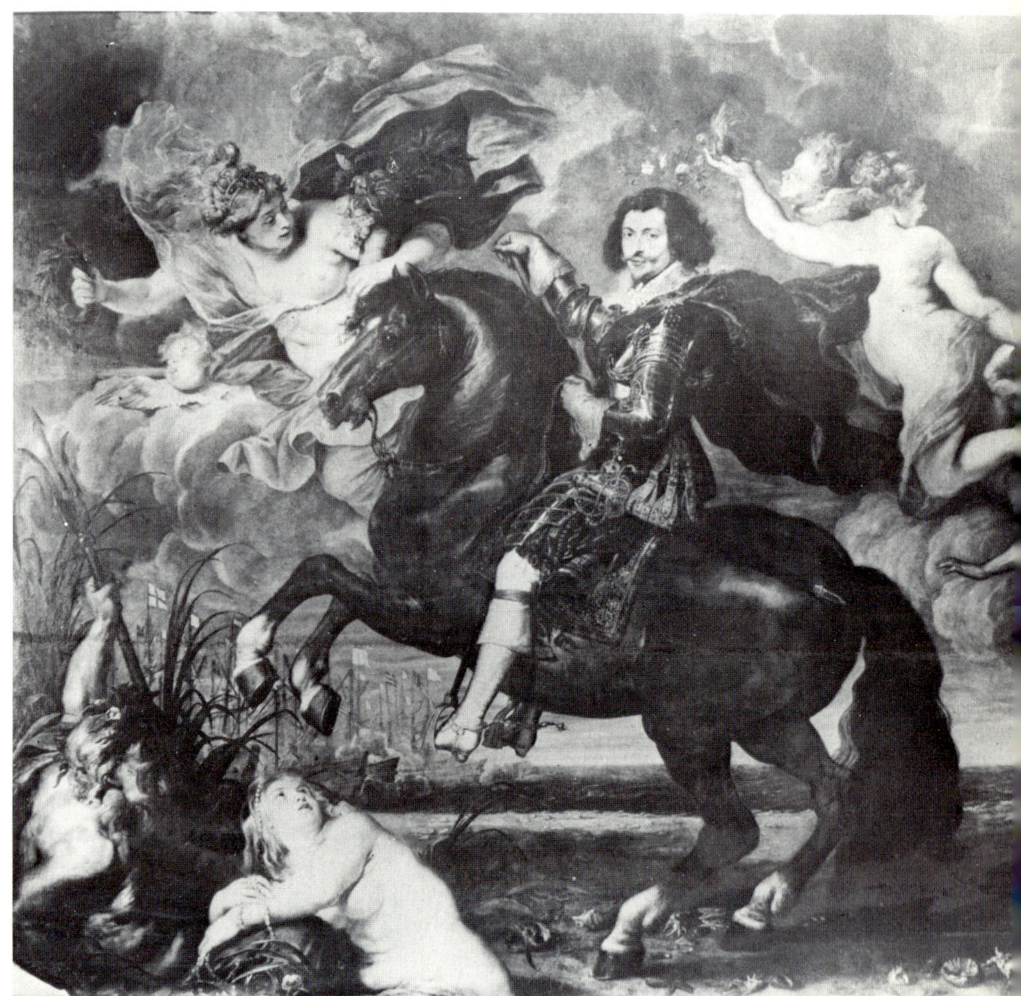

On his return to Antwerp Rubens found a scene of rejoicing for the first victory in the renewed Dutch war: the fortress of Breda had surrendered to Spinola and the Infanta had hastened to the Army to congratulate her soldiers and reward them with double pay. On her return she sat to Rubens for the portrait which, in engravings, became the official image of her to her people.

She was in her later fifties and had worn the habit of a nun ever since her husband's death. Rubens showed her as a heavily built ageing

25 *The Infanta Isabella in the habit of a nun.* Engraving by Pontius after Rubens

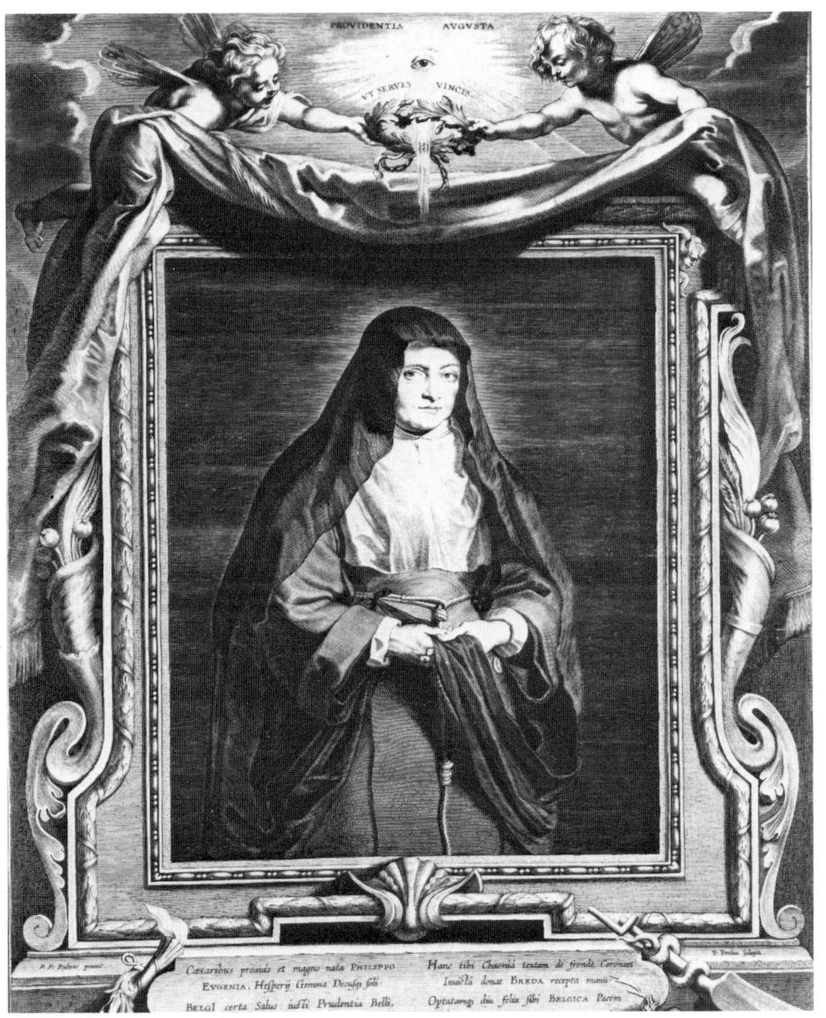

woman with no traces of conventional beauty, but her expression at once benevolent and firm, her observant eyes and judicious mouth inspire respect and confidence. 'Our Princess shows neither hate nor excessive love, but is benevolent to all,' Rubens wrote of her, and, at another time, 'She is a princess endowed with all the virtues of her sex and long experience has taught her to govern these people and remain uninfluenced by the false theories which all new-comers bring from Spain.' Her immediate visit to the troops was typical of her energy and good sense, and her simple, dignified and friendly manners endeared her to the people.

Her principal minister and adviser was Ambrogio Spinola, whom Rubens at first distrusted as a foreigner but whom he later came greatly

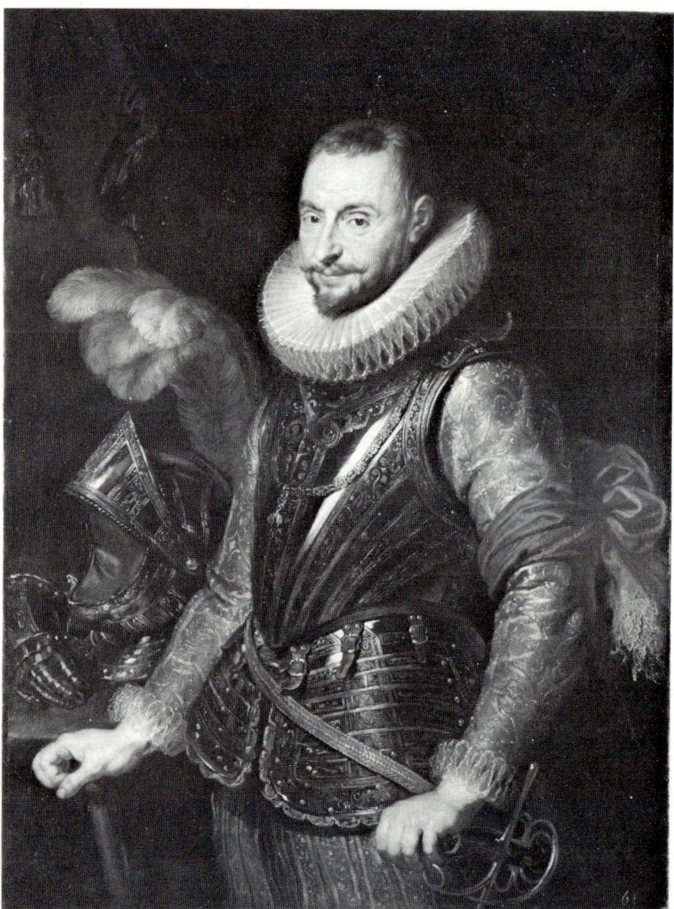

26 Rubens: *The Marquis Ambrogio Spinola*

27 Velasquez: *The Surrender of Breda*

to admire. 'He is the most prudent and sagacious man I have ever known,' he wrote, 'very cautious in all his plans; not very communicative, but rather through fear of saying too much than through lack of eloquence or spirit.' He added, a little ruefully, 'He has no taste for painting and understands no more about it than a street porter.' Spinola did, however, have his portrait painted by Rubens, standing as straight as a ramrod and not looking very communicative. Posterity will, however, always know him best as the central figure in the magnificent picture by Velasquez commemorating the surrender of Breda and painted some time after the event. Velasquez presumably saw him when he visited the Spanish Court but the figure was probably not painted from life.

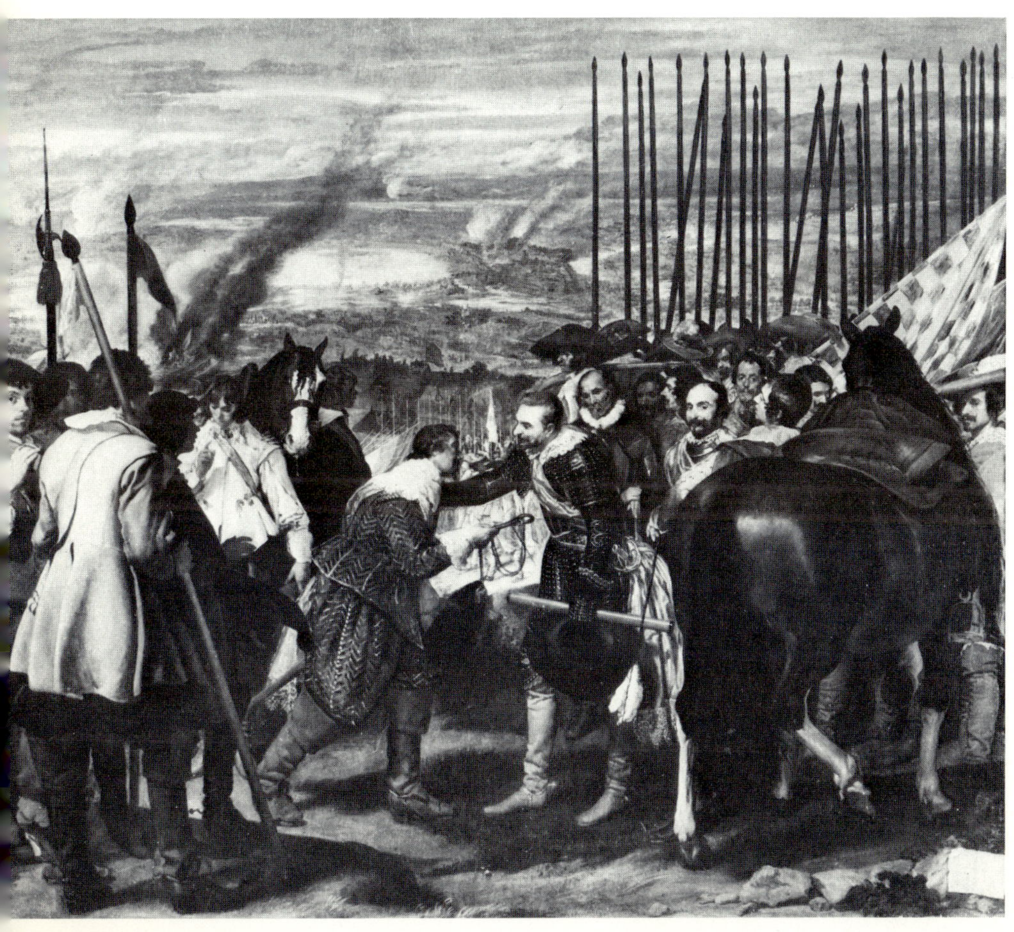

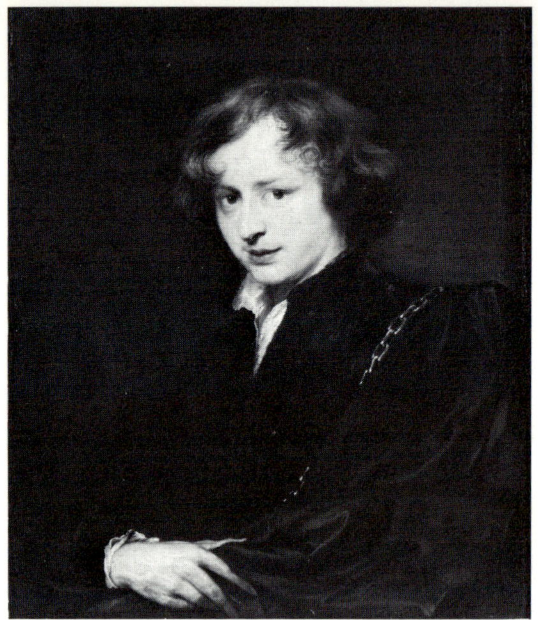

28 Van Dyck: *Self-portrait*

During the next three years the diplomatic activities of Rubens steadily increased. It is possible that the death of his beloved wife Isabella Brant, in the summer of 1626, caused him to fill his time more and more with political business as an antidote to private grief. He was still in touch with his old friend Dudley Carleton at The Hague and, in spite of Buckingham's confusing war policies, with Balthasar Gerbier. Another connoisseur and collector who was involved in the diplomatic network, the Abbé Scaglia, agent of the Duke of Savoy and a steady advocate of peace between Spain and England, was among his confidential contacts.

A painter's studio was a convenient place to arrange 'chance' meetings with visiting diplomats, but the political commitments of Rubens soon became too well known. So he used the studio of his young friend and one-time assistant Anthony Van Dyck. It was here that he organized a 'chance' meeting with the Earl of Carlisle, passing

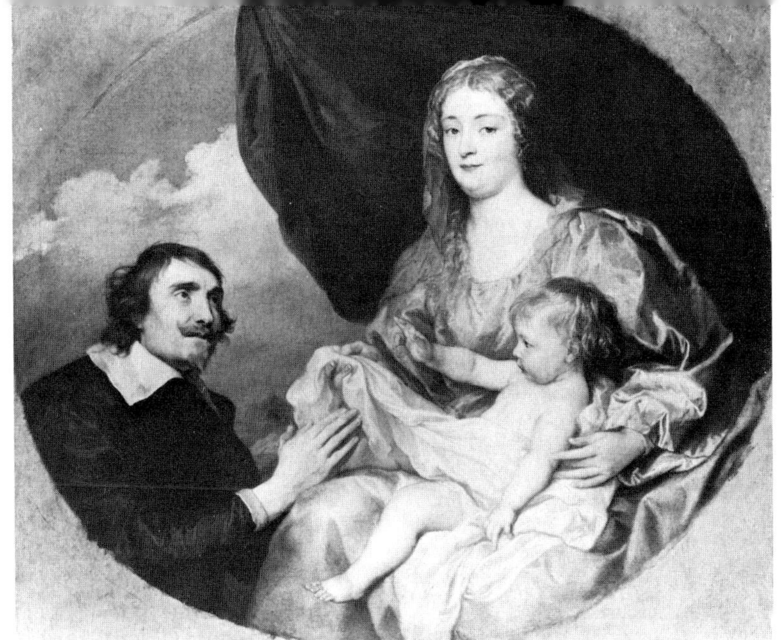

29 Van Dyck: *Virgin and
Child adored by the Abbé Scaglia*

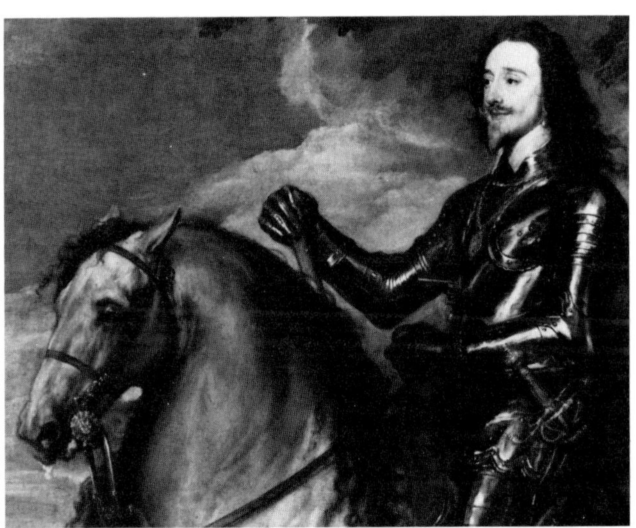

30 Van Dyck: *Equestrian
portrait of Charles I* (detail)

through Antwerp on a mission to Savoy, and used all his eloquence to persuade him that the King of England's best interests lay in a peace with Spain. Carlisle countered with an attack on Spanish duplicity and aggression that convinced Rubens he was not to be won over. But Carlisle's account of the affair shows that Rubens had done better than he knew; unconvinced of Spanish good will, Carlisle was wholly convinced of Rubens's integrity: 'He made me believe that (for his particular) nothing but good intentions and sincerity have been in his heart: which on my soul I think is true, because in other things I find him a real [i.e. reliable] man, and as well affected to the King of England's service as the King of Spain can desire.'

Rubens's heart was indeed in this matter of an Anglo-Spanish peace. Although the war in the Netherlands had at first gone very badly for the Dutch, he was well aware (as was the sagacious Spinola) that the naval superiority of the Dutch was the critical factor. They could ruin the Spanish Netherlands by their continuous blockade of the Scheldt. Antwerp was the first and principal sufferer: 'Our city goes step by step to ruin,' Rubens wrote a month or two after his interview with Carlisle.

As a devoted citizen of Antwerp, and also as an inheritor of the great cultural tradition of the Netherlands, he wanted above all to see North and South reunited, not by conquest, but through some kind of federal solution. That such a solution would be under the suzerainty of the Spanish Crown seemed to him legitimate and natural; the Spanish King was the lineal heir of the great Dukes of Burgundy under whom the civilization of the Netherlands had reached its peak. This solution could surely be achieved in such a way as to leave almost complete independence to the various provinces in running their own affairs and practising their own religions. He could never bring himself to believe that the Dutch would not accept this.

Yet an exploratory visit to the Dutch Republic, in which Gerbier had joined him, had no political results at all. He had gone under cover of visiting the northern artists and had both enjoyed and profited by that part of his visit, especially the time he had spent in Utrecht with Gerard

40

Honthorst. Honthorst had lived many years in Rome where he had earned considerable respect with his night-pieces – Gherardo della Notte, they called him. But on his return to Holland he had been appointed Court painter to the sister of Charles I, the exiled Queen of Bohemia. Since the Queen's little Court at The Hague was an active centre for the Protestant Cause in the Thirty Years War, I find it hard to believe that Honthorst himself was not in some way involved in the secret diplomacy of this epoch. But this question does not seem to have been investigated.

However that may be, the mission of Rubens had no result, and I date from its failure his ardent and increasing conviction that, once Spain and England made peace, the English could bring pressure to bear on the Dutch. It sounded feasible: the English under Elizabeth I had given active help to the Dutch in the earlier part of the war. The attitude of her two successors, James I and Charles I, was very much cooler, as neither of them approved of Republicans or rebels, but the alliance had still been maintained and English volunteers formed no inconsiderable part of the Dutch forces.

31 Gerard Honthorst:
Christ before Caiaphas

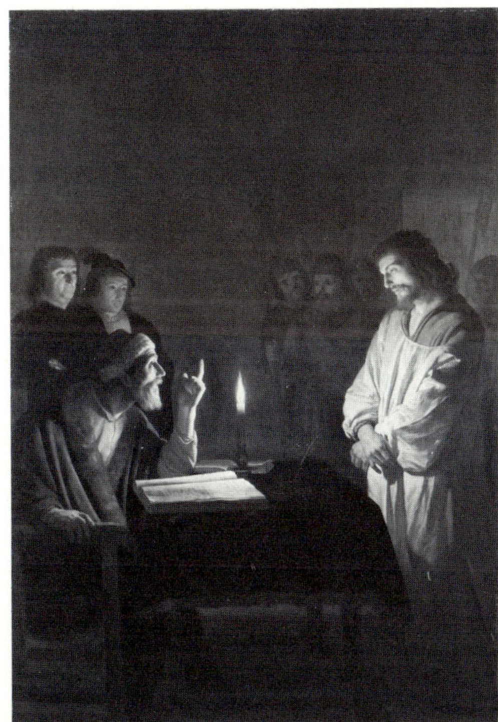

By 1627, when Rubens renewed his contacts with Buckingham through Gerbier, it looked as though the volatile Duke himself might be willing to work for peace with Spain so as to prosecute the war against France more effectively. But the cautious negotiations of Rubens and the hopes of the Infanta and Spinola were dashed by the folly of Olivares, first minister to the King of Spain, who was hoodwinked by Richelieu into signing a treaty with France for a joint attack on England. No doubt this looked reasonable to him as England was at war with both of them, but the more experienced Spinola, the Infanta – and of course Rubens – saw at once that Richelieu's aim was only to neutralize Spain while he was temporarily hampered by a Huguenot revolt in France.

'We believe', Rubens wrote to Gerbier, 'that this alliance will be like thunder without lightning, making a noise in the air without effect.' He went on to emphasize 'the perfidy of the French' and the known fact that they were assisting the Dutch. 'The Infanta and the Marquis [Spinola] are determined to continue our negotiations [for peace with England] believing that the agreement between France and Spain will have no effect and will not last. All intelligent men here, both clergy and laity, laugh at it. . . .'

Neither the Infanta nor Spinola thought it a mere laughing matter, and Spinola left soon after to remonstrate in person with the Court at Madrid. Here he persuaded the King to allow Rubens to go on with his exploratory approaches to England, and ultimately in the late summer of 1628 Rubens himself was summoned to Madrid to put the case for an Anglo-Spanish treaty before King and Council. The Infanta from the first knew that no better envoy could be chosen when the time was ripe to approach the King of England in person and after some delay this was agreed in Spain.

In the meantime Buckingham had been assassinated, an event which made peace more, rather than less, likely, as King Charles had taken his warlike tone largely from the favourite; he himself was more inclined to a quiet life, especially after the humiliating defeats he had suffered in the war and at the hands of a formidably critical House of Commons.

42

Rubens stayed seven months in Madrid from September 1628 to April 1629 and, in spite of a painful attack of gout (his first) and the long delays that occurred before his mission to England was finally settled, he profited to the utmost by his visit. He painted portraits of all the Royal Family to send to the Infanta in Brussels, he altered and improved an *Adoration of the Magi* he had painted nearly twenty years earlier and which he now found lodged in the Royal Collection, and he copied the superb Titians which were the pride and joy of the Spanish King. He also took an interest in the young Court painter Velasquez. On his earlier visit to Spain in 1603 he had found no native painter to admire, but he was deeply impressed by Velasquez and persuaded the King to give the brilliant young man leave of absence to widen his artistic horizon in Rome.

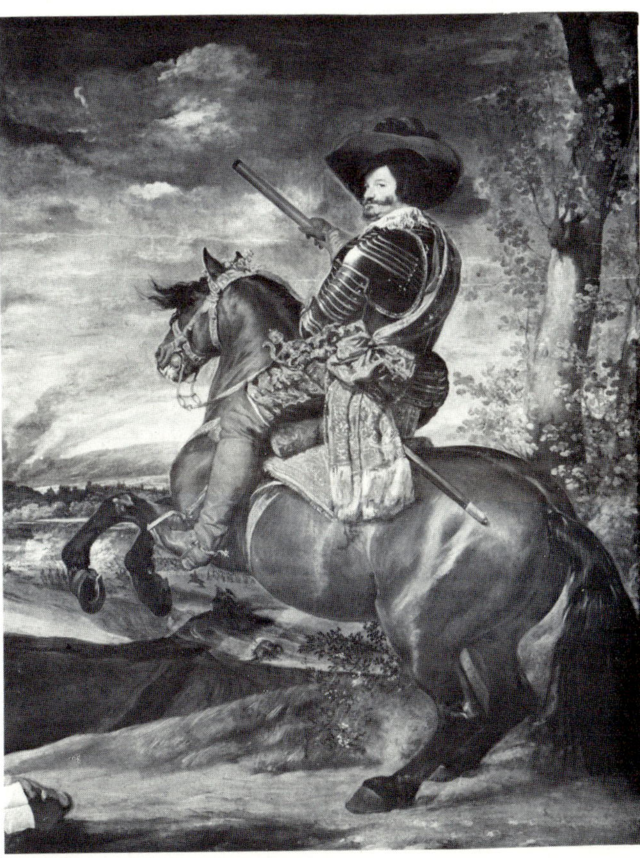

32 Velasquez: *Equestrian portrait of Count Olivares*

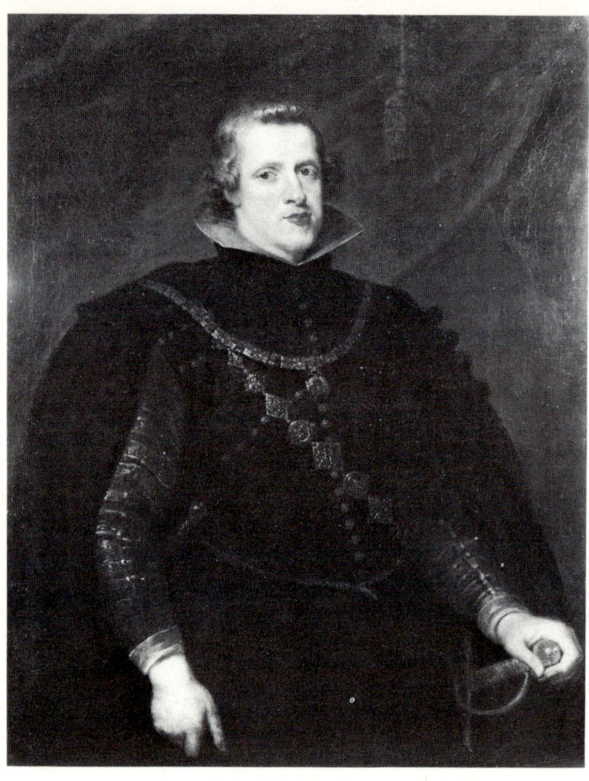

33 Rubens: *Philip IV*

He came to take a fatherly interest in the twenty-three-year-old
Philip IV who turned to him with exceptional friendship. 'He really
takes an extreme delight in painting . . .', wrote Rubens, 'I know him
already by personal contact, for since I have a room in the Palace he
comes to see me almost every day. . . . He is endowed by nature with all
the gifts of body and spirit . . . and would be capable of governing under
any conditions, were it not that he mistrusts himself and defers too much
to others. . . .'

The chief minister Olivares was, according to his lights, an honest
and responsible minister, and Rubens came almost to pity him for the
hatred to which he was exposed in an envious Court. When the Dutch
admiral Piet Hein captured the entire Spanish silver fleet off the coast

44

of Cuba, Rubens was shocked at the comments of the courtiers: 'The loss of the fleet has caused great discussion. . . . It is imputed to folly and negligence rather than misfortune since no precautions were taken in spite of timely warnings. . . . Almost [everyone] here [is] very glad about it, feeling that this public calamity can be set down as a disgrace to their rulers. . . . So great is the power of hate that they overlook their own ills for the mere pleasure of vengeance.'

Late in April 1629 Rubens was at last able to leave Madrid with his credentials. Pausing only briefly in the Netherlands, he landed at Dover towards the middle of June. When he left again in March 1630 he had secured peace and friendship between England and Spain, and it remained only for the noble ambassador specially appointed for the purpose to sign the treaty.

The political details of his interviews with Charles I and with Sir Francis Cottington, who was in effect the foreign minister, are complex without being particularly interesting. The French and Venetian ambassadors were hostile and did what they could to obstruct, but Rubens had an ally in the Duke of Savoy's representative. All these reactions reflected the current relations, friendly or otherwise, of the European powers – relations on the whole ephemeral and egotistical.

More interesting than the diplomatic problems which Rubens skil-fully negotiated are his comments on the English scene. Naturally he got on well with the King. Charles, who had expressed his desire 'to know a person of such merit', was not disappointed. Neither was Rubens. His dispatches to Olivares describe the remarkably free inter-change of views between the shy and often tongue-tied King and the persuasive painter-diplomat. With Rubens Charles became talkative, even to the point of indiscretion: 'He said he detested the French and had never trusted them . . .', an odd admission considering his French marriage alliance. He also dropped more than a hint that he disliked his own entanglement with the Protestant side in the German war (in spite of the fact that his only sister was married to one of the principal protagonists) and he made no secret of his disapproval of the Dutch as rebels against their legal sovereign.

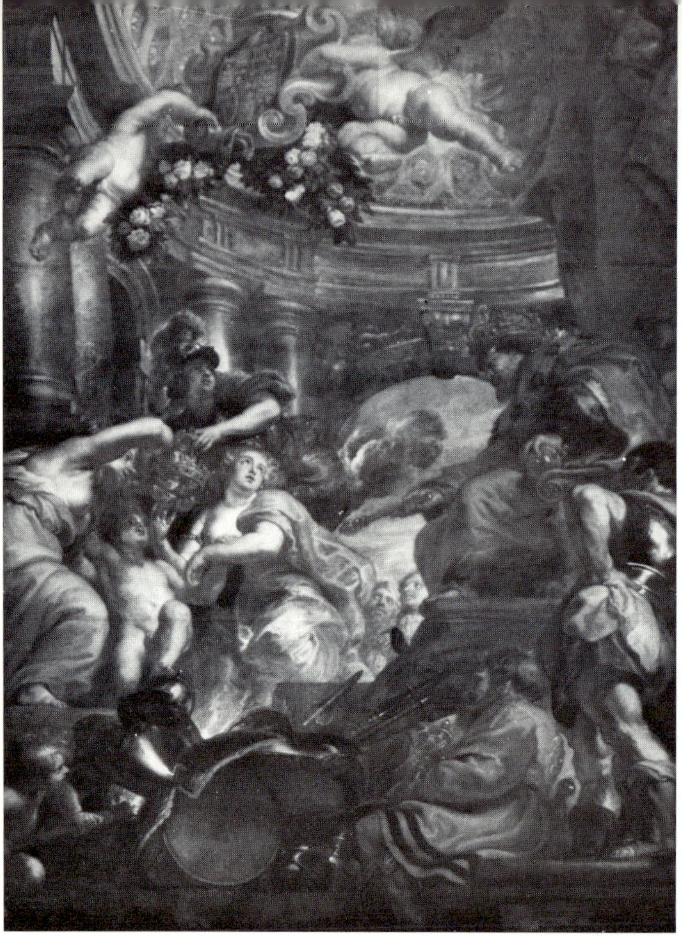

34 Rubens: *Union of England and Scotland*
Part of ceiling of Banqueting House,
Whitehall, London

35 Anon: *Sir Francis Cottington*

46

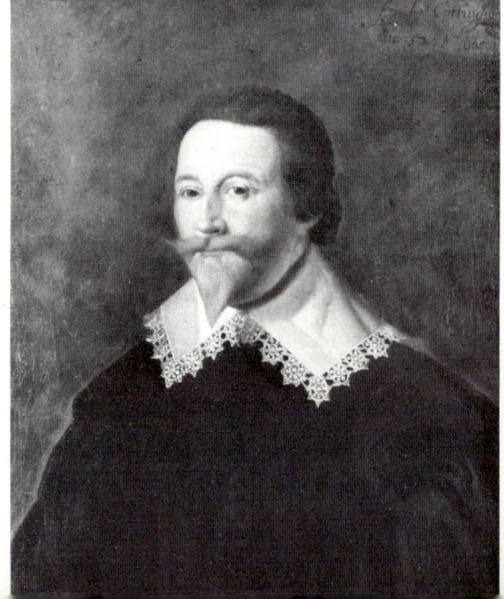

The King and the painter must also have talked much about pictures but this, unhappily, was not a matter that Rubens included in his dispatches. It was during this visit to England that he concluded a business first mooted nearly ten years before – namely that he should paint the ceiling of the great new Banqueting House which Inigo Jones was building for the King in Whitehall. The subject for the pictures was to be the peace and prosperity of the reign of the late King James. If the King himself was hardly an inspiring figure, the subject was one after Rubens's own heart and he could sincerely honour a monarch who had tried, however unsuccessfully, to be the peacemaker of Europe.

Rubens said on the whole little about Charles's character but singled out 'constancy and equanimity' as his best qualities. He was, however, puzzled by the apparent dependence of the King on his ministers for all final decisions: 'For whereas in other Courts negotiations begin with the ministers and finish with the Royal word and signature, here they begin with the King and end with the ministers.'

As to the Court itself, he clearly found the atmosphere less poisonous than at Madrid, but was shocked by the expenditure of the nobility, whom he thought the most extravagant in Europe. Since he knew the nobility of France, Spain and Italy as well as the Netherlands this opinion is worthy of notice:

All the leading nobles live on a sumptuous scale and spend money lavishly so that the majority of them are hopelessly in debt. Among these in the first place are the Earl of Carlisle and the Earl of Holland who, by their fine table, maintain their following and their position among the nobility, since splendour and liberality are the first considerations at this Court. I do not speak of the many other lords and ministers who, for the most part, have inadequate revenues to support their rank ... that is why public and private interests are sold here for ready money. And I know from reliable sources that Cardinal Richelieu is very liberal and most experienced in gaining partisans in this manner.

As he was writing to Olivares, Rubens said nothing of partisans gained for Spain by exactly the same means. He himself had a reliable ally in the amiable Hispanophile Sir Francis Cottington who was largely instrumental in the success of the treaty. Ruined by the Civil War, Cottington would ultimately die, a Catholic, in Valladolid: urbane and imperturbable to the last.

In England, as in Spain, Rubens spent his enforced leisure in painting and in going to see works of art. He was amazed at what he found. Writing to his friend Pierre Dupuy, the Royal librarian in Paris, he described England as 'worthy of the interest of every gentleman, not only for the beauty of the countryside and the charm of the nation, not only for the splendour of its outward culture, which seems to be extreme, as of a people rich and happy in the lap of peace, but also for the great quantity of fine pictures, statues and ancient inscriptions which are to be found in this Court.'

Rubens elaborated the same theme to his friend Fabri de Peiresc:

In this island I find none of the crudeness which one might expect from a place so remote from Italian elegance . . . and when it comes to fine pictures by the hands of the greatest masters, I have never seen such a large number in one place as in the Royal Palace and in the Gallery of the late Duke of Buckingham. The Earl of Arundel possesses a countless number of ancient statues and Greek and Latin inscriptions. . . .

He went on to regret that the distinguished antiquary John Selden, who had transcribed and described Arundel's inscriptions, had been one of the King's foremost critics in the recent Parliament and was now under arrest.

Some of the pictures which Rubens saw were already known to him, as King Charles had bought almost the entire collection of the bankrupt Duke of Mantua, son of his first patron.

During his stay in England, he lodged at the house of his old friend Gerbier whose wife and children he painted. He painted the children again in that splendid composition, now in the National Gallery, the *Allegory of Peace and War*. Here Gerbier's little daughters figure as the happy beneficiaries of peace and plenty, while the goddess Minerva firmly guides the war god Mars away from the festive scene. Rubens presented this picture to the King.

48

36 Studio of Rubens: *The Gerbier family*

37 Rubens: *Allegory of Peace and War*

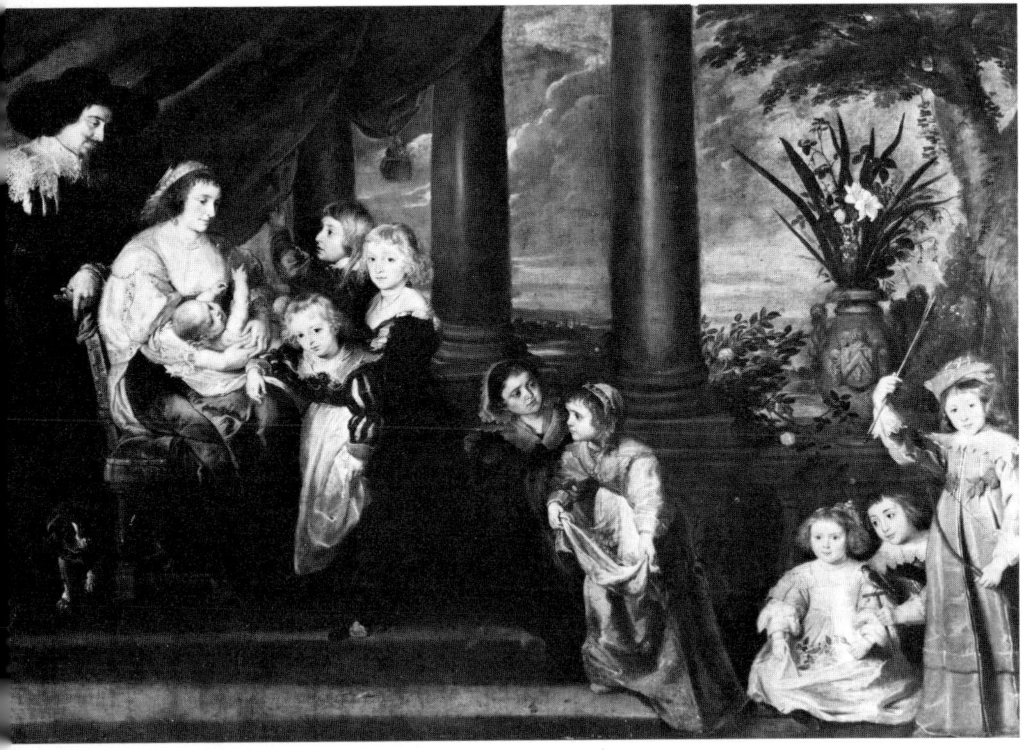

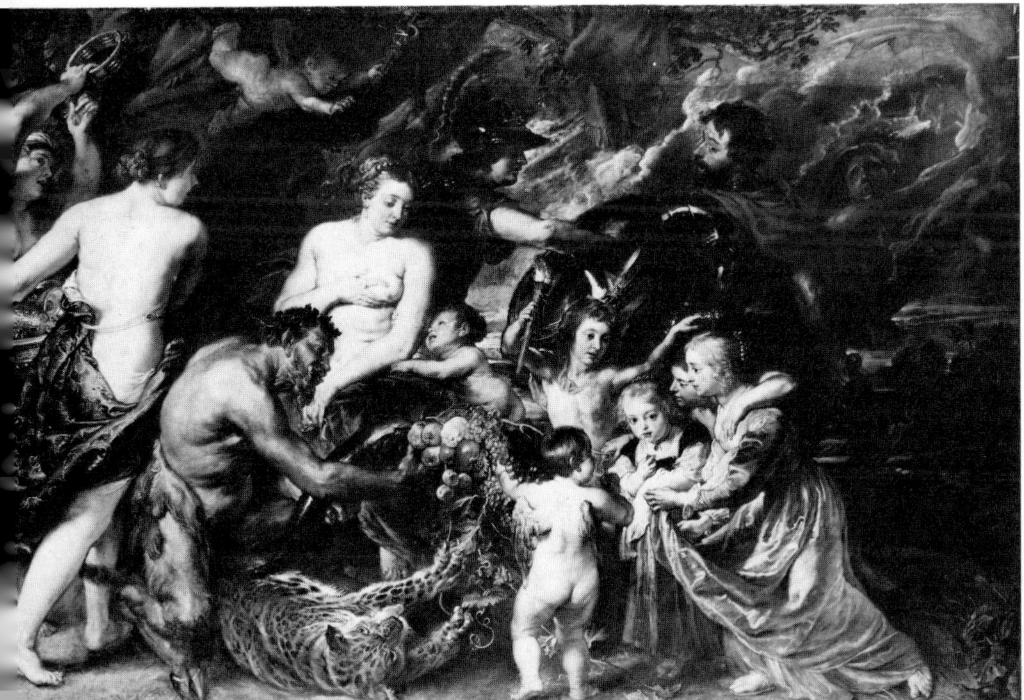

38 Rubens: *St George and the Dragon*

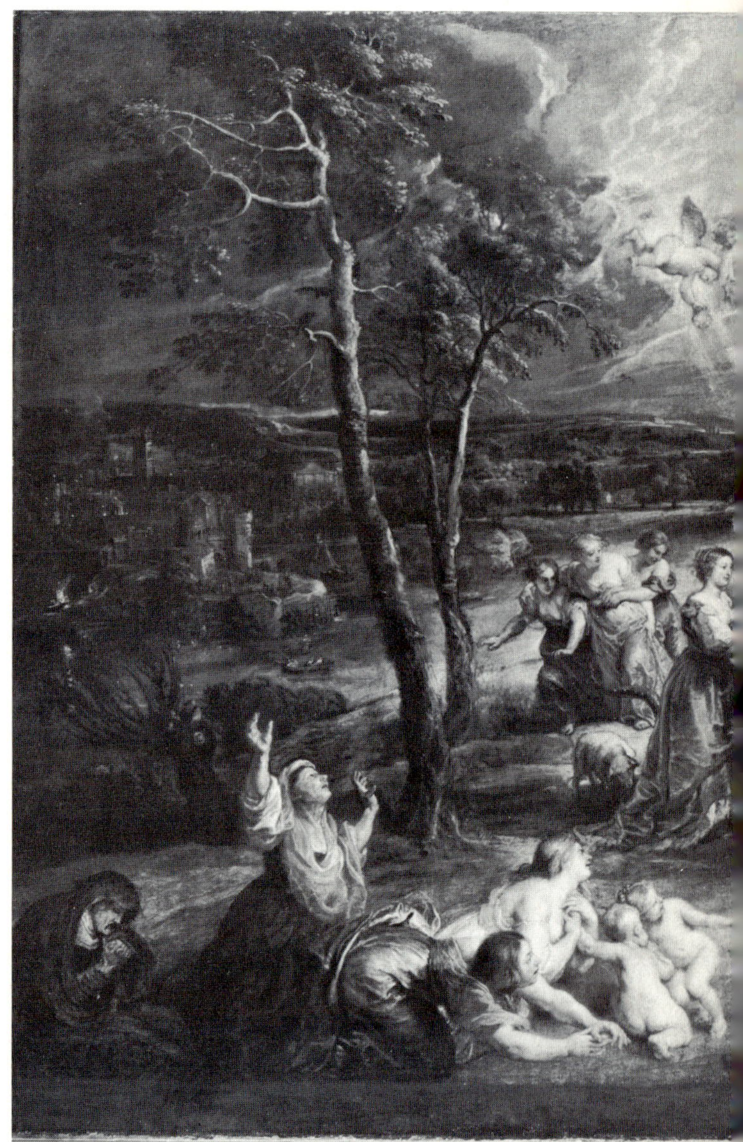

He also painted a *St George and the Dragon* in which the warrior saint somewhat resembles Charles I, the rescued princess a Rubenesque Henrietta Maria, and the whole scene is set against a view of the Thames below Greenwich. Although the painting is now in the Royal Collection, it belonged first to the connoisseur courtier Endymion Porter who perhaps acquired it from Rubens.

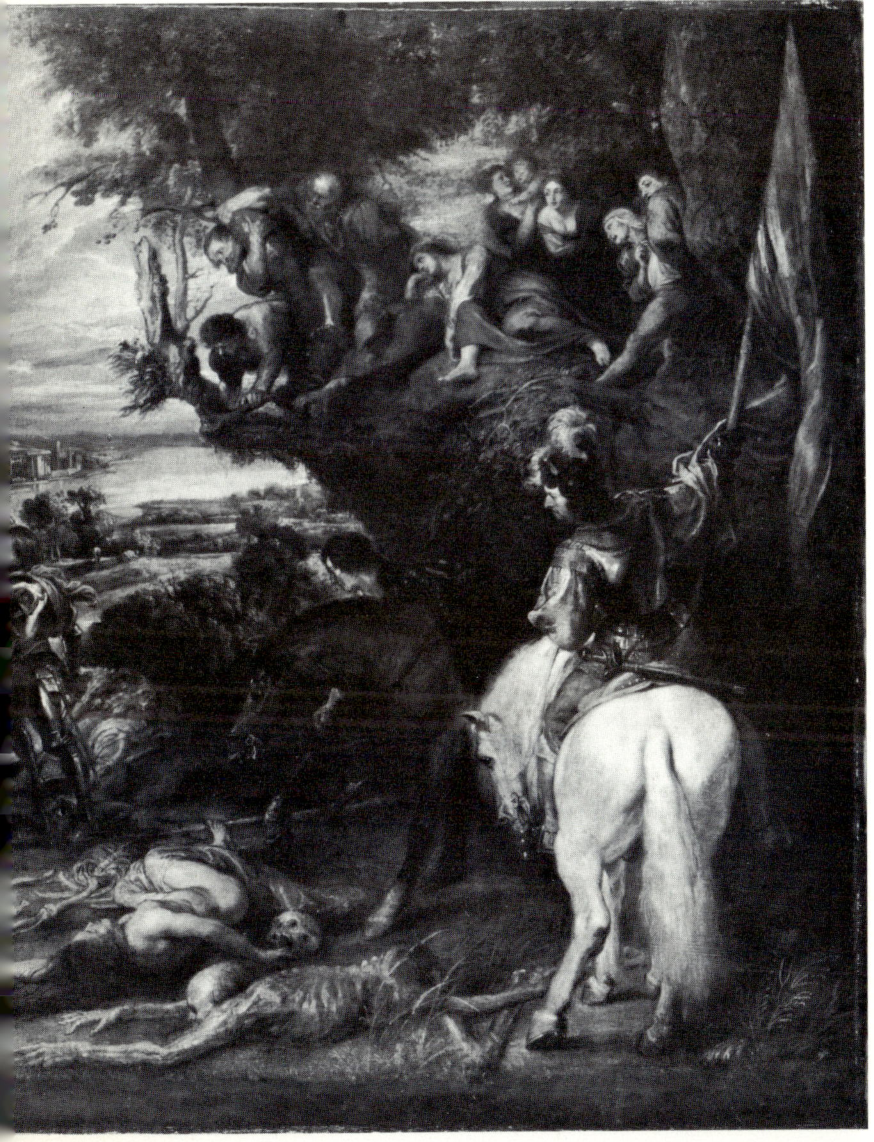

The summit of Rubens's diplomatic career proved to be also his most tragic disappointment. Before leaving England, he called on the venerable Dutch statesman Albert Joachimi who had been for many years the resident ambassador. We have only indirect knowledge of what took place between them, but Rubens presumably represented the Anglo-Spanish treaty as a step towards the peaceful reunion of the Netherlands, and may have suggested English mediation towards that (to him) desirable end. Since the reunion that Rubens envisaged would have involved the Dutch in recognition of the King of Spain's sovereignty, Joachimi rejected the suggestion outright. The Netherlands, he argued, could only be reunited if the South joined with the North to drive the Spaniards out: an answer which must have made it clear to Rubens that the peace for which he had worked and hoped was as far off as ever.

Rubens had failed in his ultimate objective and though he was still from time to time during the next ten years employed on further fruitless negotiations with the Dutch, his dominating interest and absorbing occupation after his return from England to Antwerp was his painting.

In December 1630 he married Hélène Fourment, the youngest daughter of an Antwerp merchant, his neighbour and friend. She was sixteen; he was fifty-three, but the marriage seems to have been as happy as it was fruitful. His unfinished painting of Hélène and her children, now in the Louvre, shows her with a face of simple, rapt contentment.

Soon after his marriage he bought the Château de Steen, the pleasant country house where, as he grew older, he spent all the time he could spare from his Antwerp studio. But he had immense commissions to fulfil, first of all the pictures for Whitehall which are to this day its glory and its pride. He had too an order for a long series of classical scenes wanted by Philip IV for his hunting lodge, Torre de la Parada – a series on which he was still working at the time of his death. Some of his most fresh and beautiful mythological pieces date from this last decade and the rejuvenating influence of his young wife is suggested by the frequent appearance in them of a figure which resembles her.

39 Rubens: *Hélène Fourment in her wedding dress*

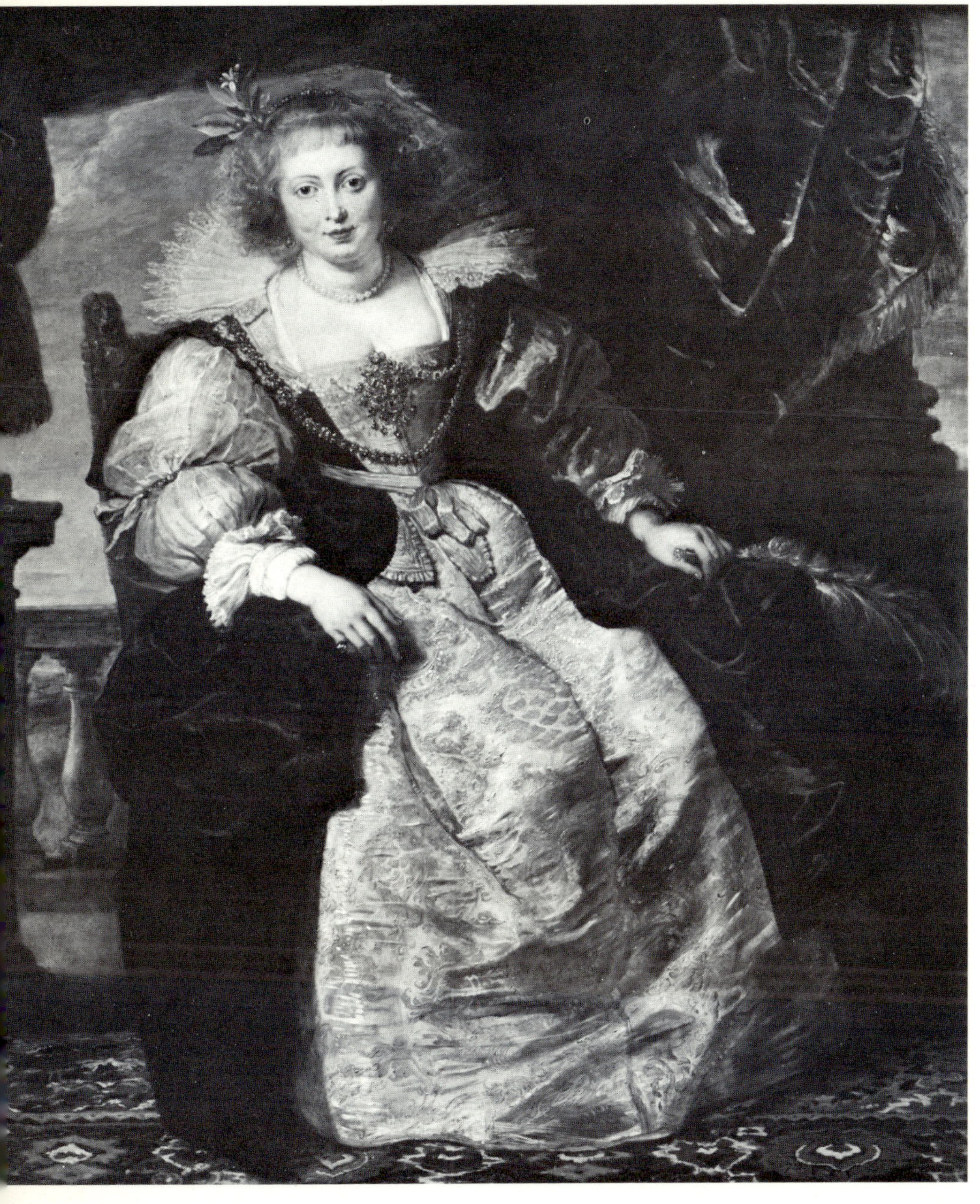

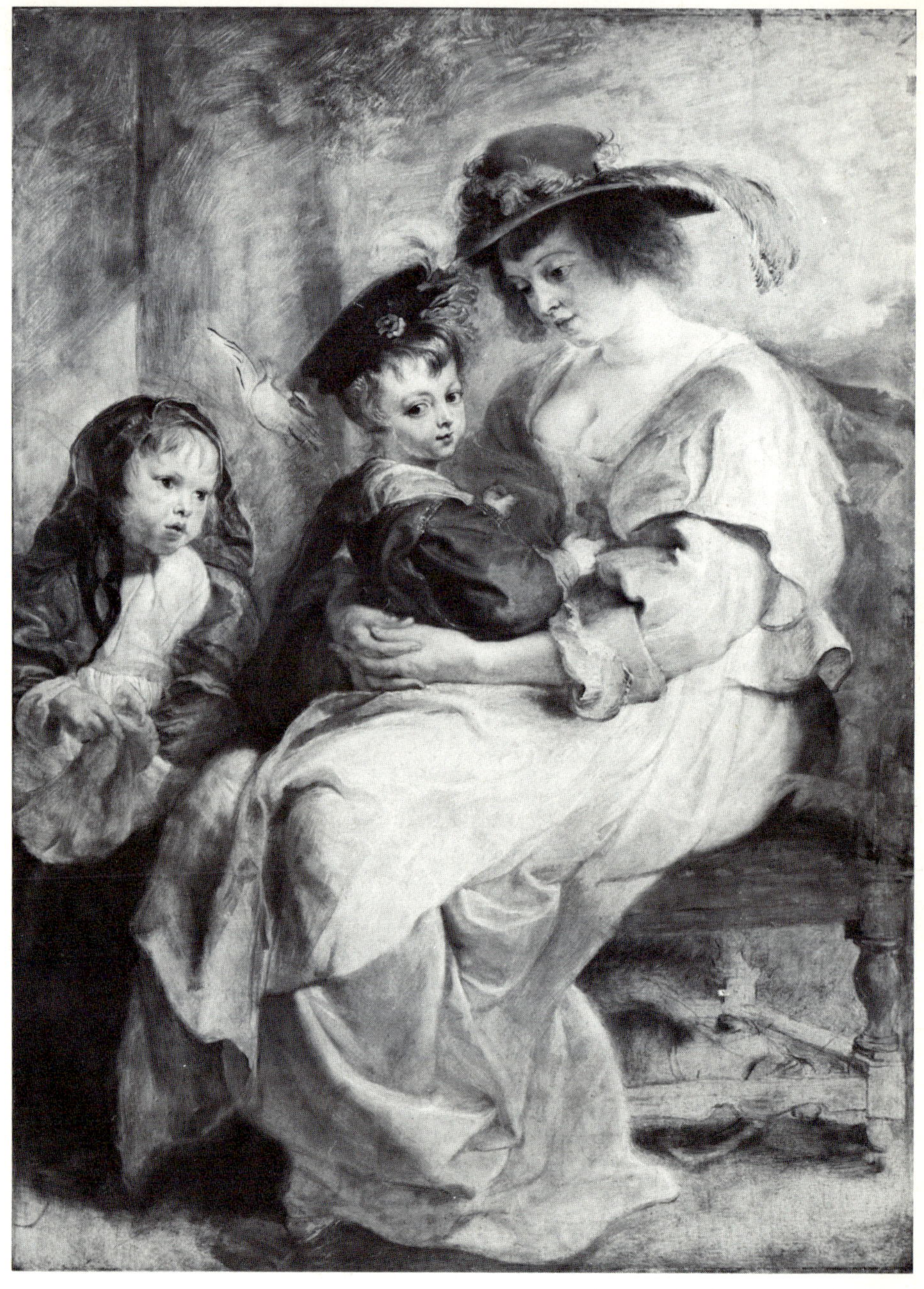

40 Rubens: *Hélène Fourment with her children*

41 Rubens: *The Artist with Hélène Fourment and his son Nicholas, walking in their garden in Antwerp*

42 Rubens: *Autumn landscape with a view of the Château de Steen*

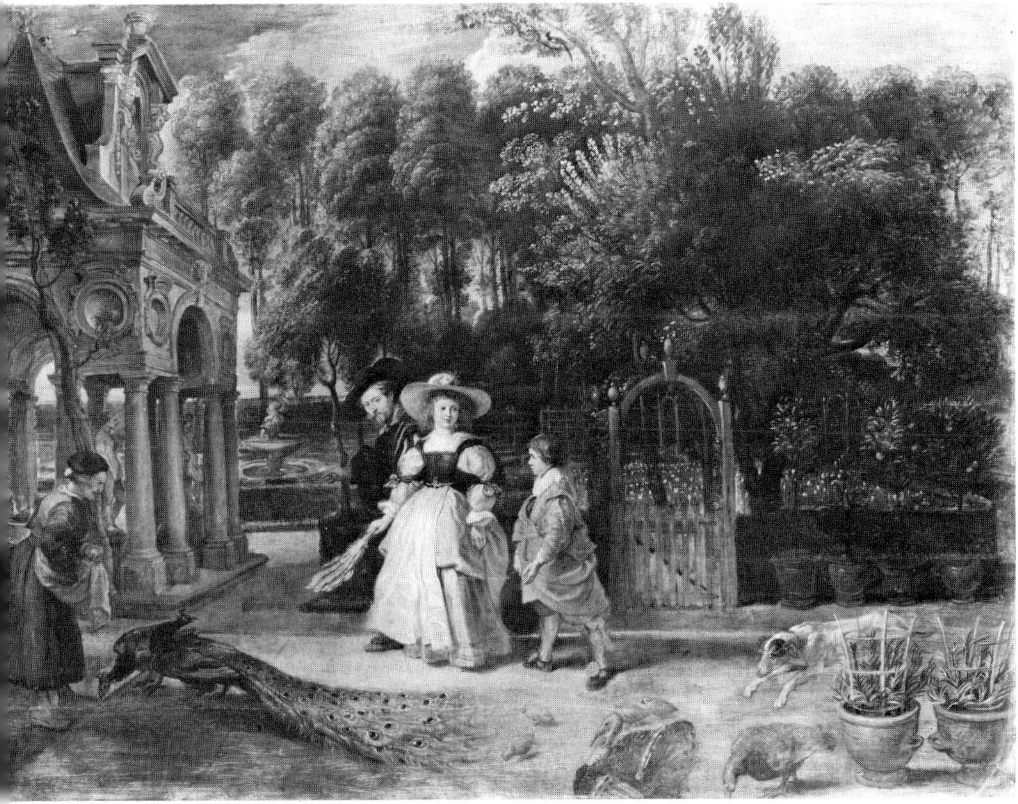

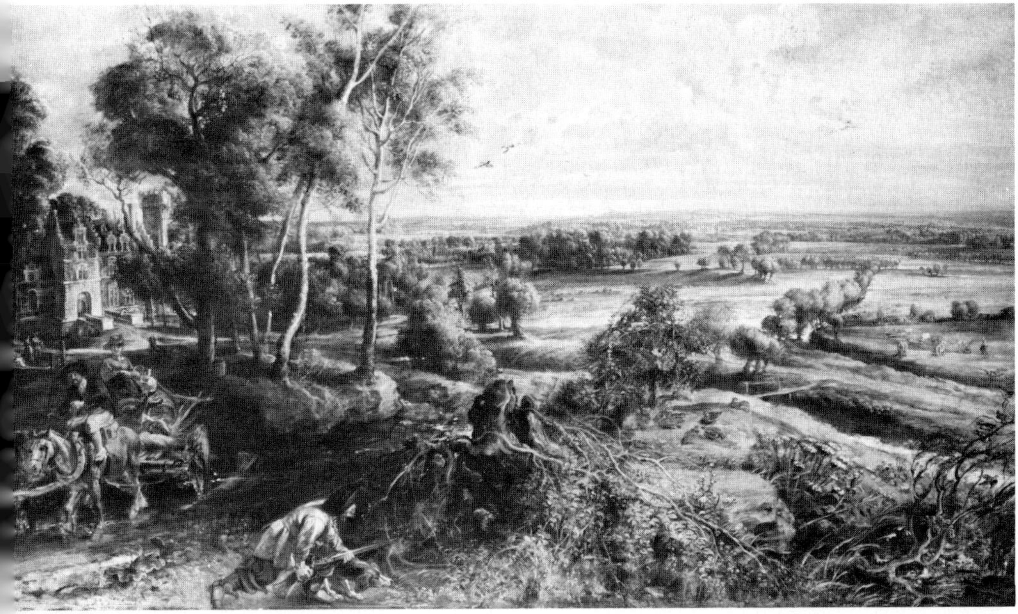

43 Rubens: *Self-portrait*

44 Rubens's house in Antwerp

45 Interior of Rubens's house in Antwerp

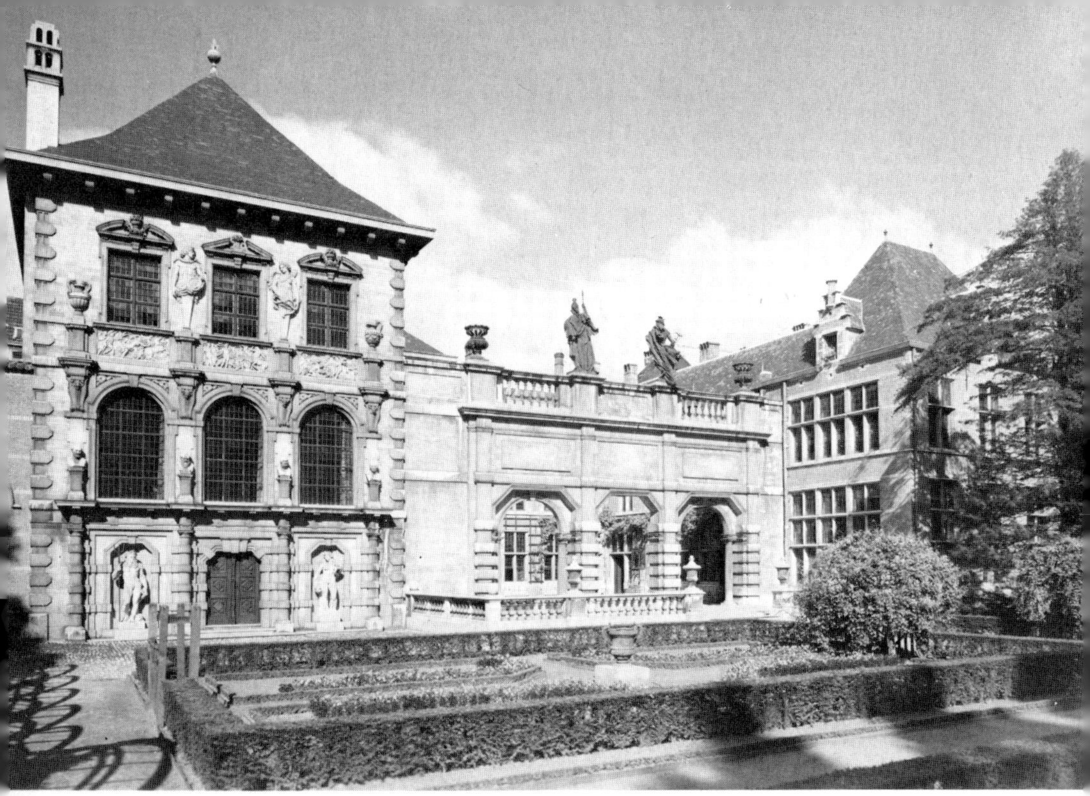

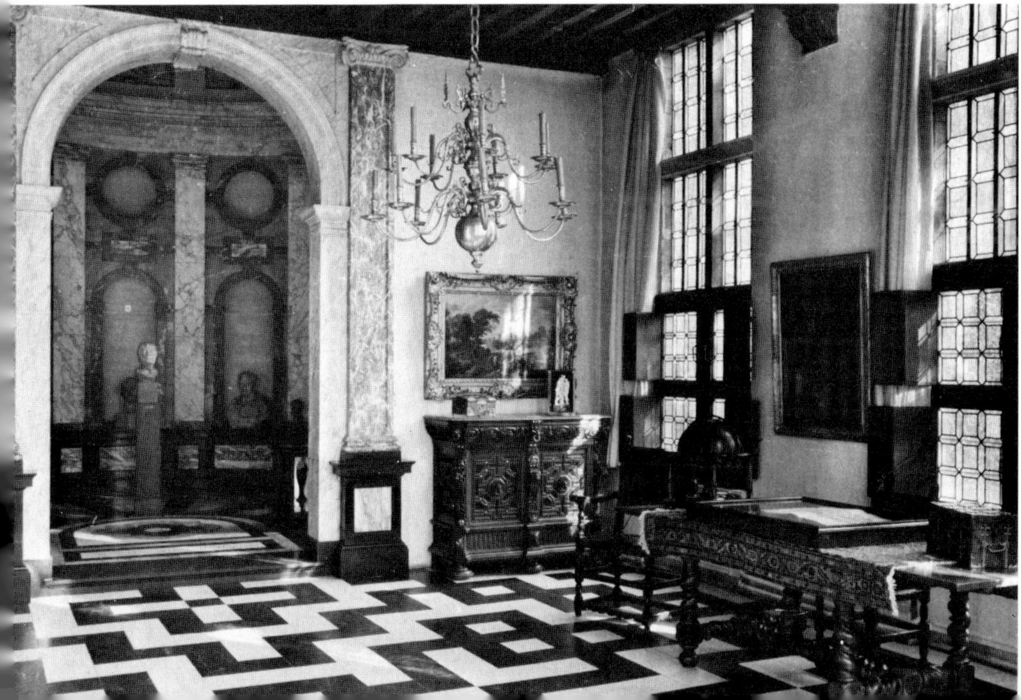

In December 1633 died the Infanta whom he had so long served and
honoured. She was succeeded as Governor by the younger brother of
Philip IV, the Cardinal-Infante Ferdinand, an able and active soldier
with nothing of the Churchman about him. He reached the Netherlands fresh from a campaign in Germany where, at Nördlingen, he and
his Austrian allies had inflicted a shattering defeat on the Swedish and
Protestant forces. This victory for some years tilted the balance of
Europe once again in favour of the Catholic Habsburg powers, with

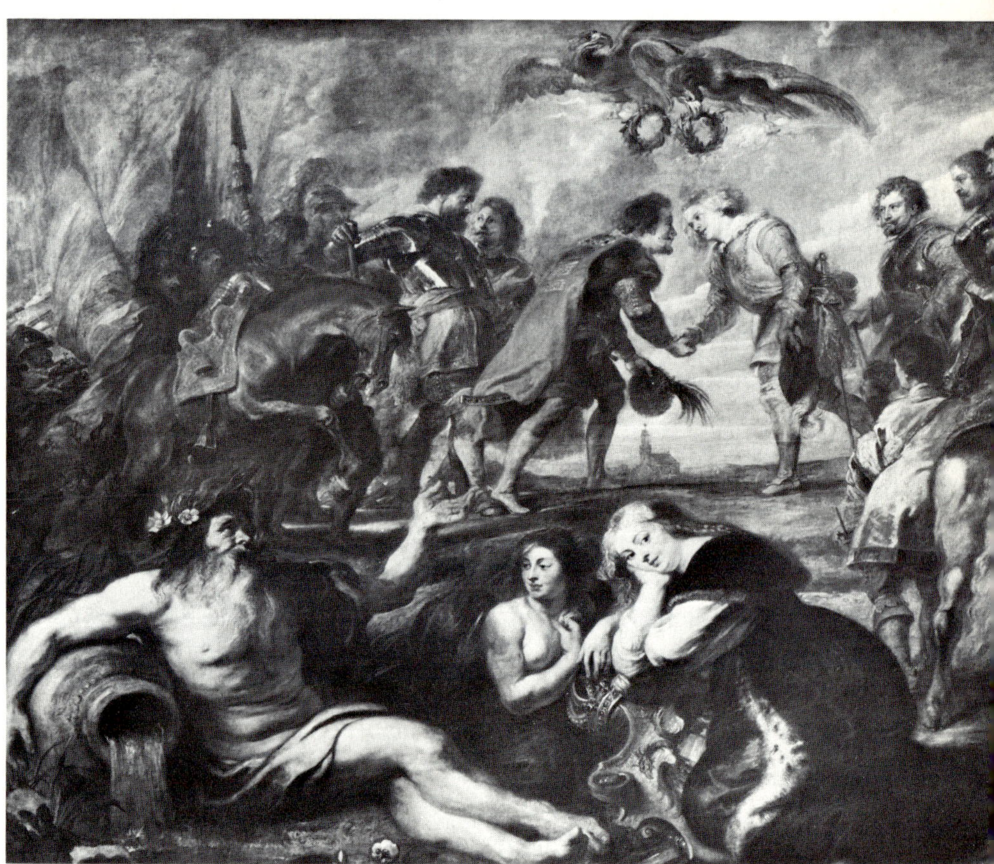

consequent encouragement to the hard-pressed Spanish Netherlands.

Rubens designed triumphal arches which greeted the entry of the Cardinal-Infante to Antwerp. But among the lavish tributes to the young man's victory and the feats of his ancestors, he included an allegory imploring his assistance for the impoverished and decaying city of Antwerp. He was fortunate that the renewed atmosphere of hope inaugurated by the Battle of Nördlingen did not altogether fade before his death in 1640.

46 Rubens: *Meeting of Cardinal-Infante Ferdinand and Ferdinand, King of Hungary, at the Battle of Nördlingen, 2 September, 1634*

47 Rubens: *Cardinal-Infante Ferdinand*

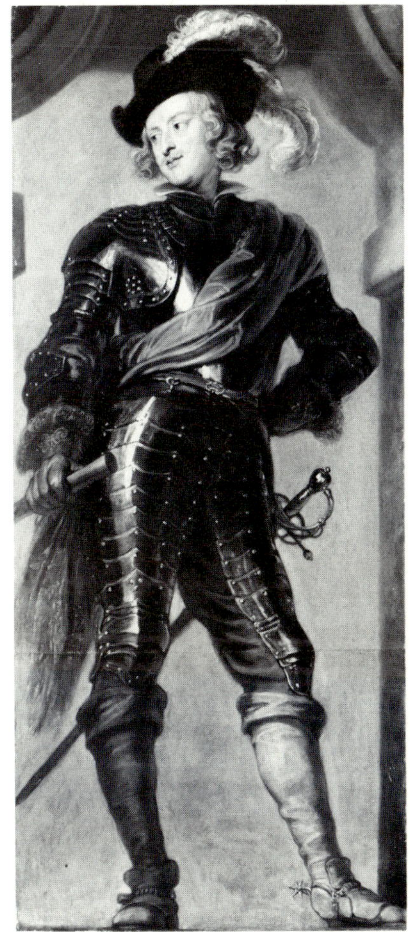

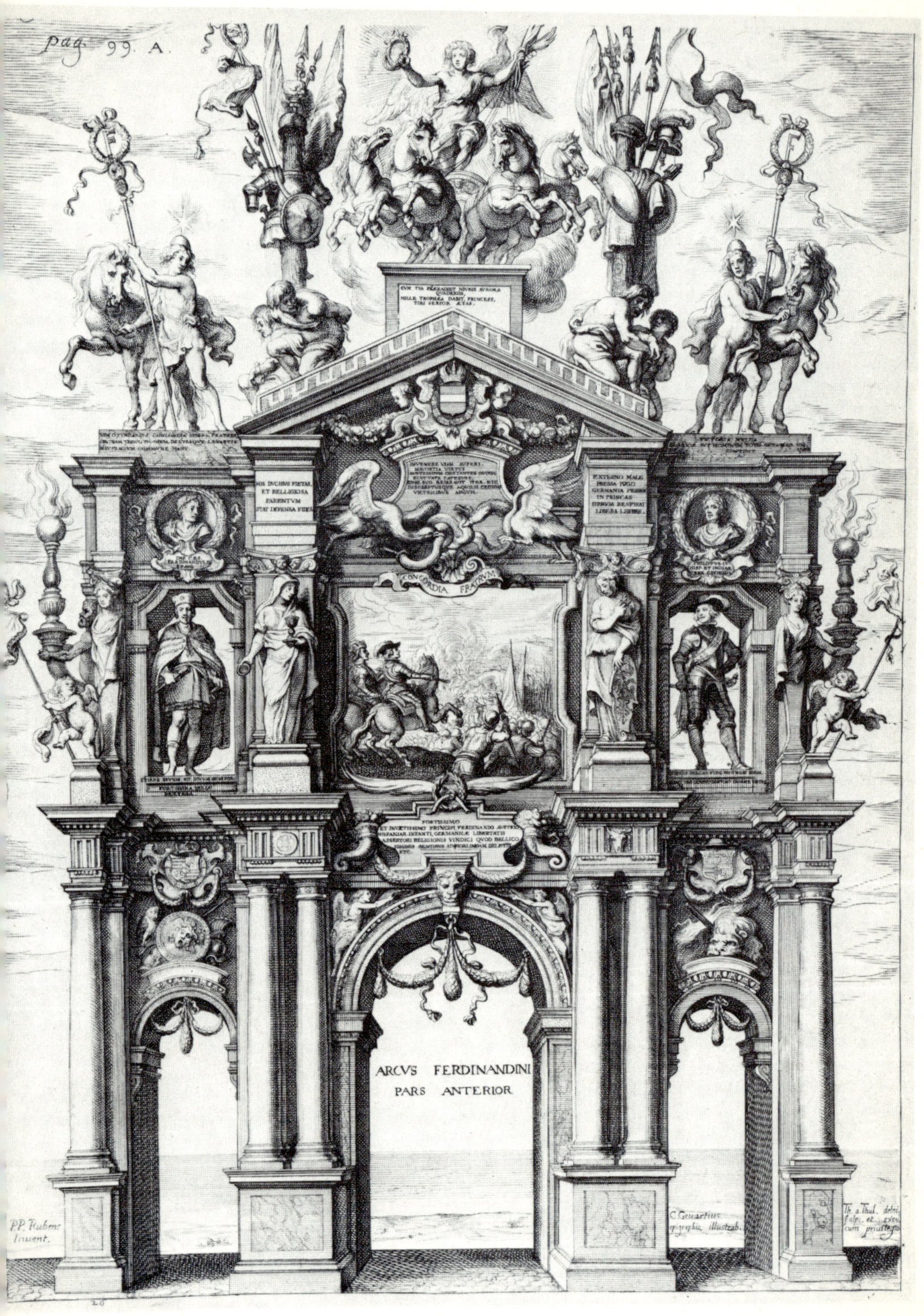
ARCVS FERDINANDINI
PARS ANTERIOR
P.P. Rubens
Inuent.
C. Gevartius
epigraphe illustrab.
Th. a Thul. delin.
sculp. et excud.
cum privilegio

In the last years his family, his friends and his painting filled his life. Even the gout, which sometimes crippled his right hand, never inter/ rupted his work for long. It was in these years, at the Château de Steen, that he devoted himself for his own pleasure to painting the gentle domestic landscape of his home, seeking to capture the infinite varia/ tions of light over the flat, watery, fertile fields.

His achievement as a diplomat, though worthy of respect for its motives and its integrity, is little more than a footnote to his career as a painter. Nevertheless he brought to it, as he brought to his painting, undiscouraged perseverance, resilient patience, acute observation and a continuously active commitment to the living world. In his last years his love for, and interest in, all created things found its last and calmest outlet in his landscape painting. After all, the passage of the seasons and the eternal sequence of sunrise and sunset encompass and outlast all that man achieves – in politics or in paint.

48 Front face of Arch of Ferdinand. Etching by T. van Thulden for
Gervasius's *Pompa introitus Ferdinandi* (Antwerp 1641–42)

49 Rubens: *Landscape with a shepherd and his flock*

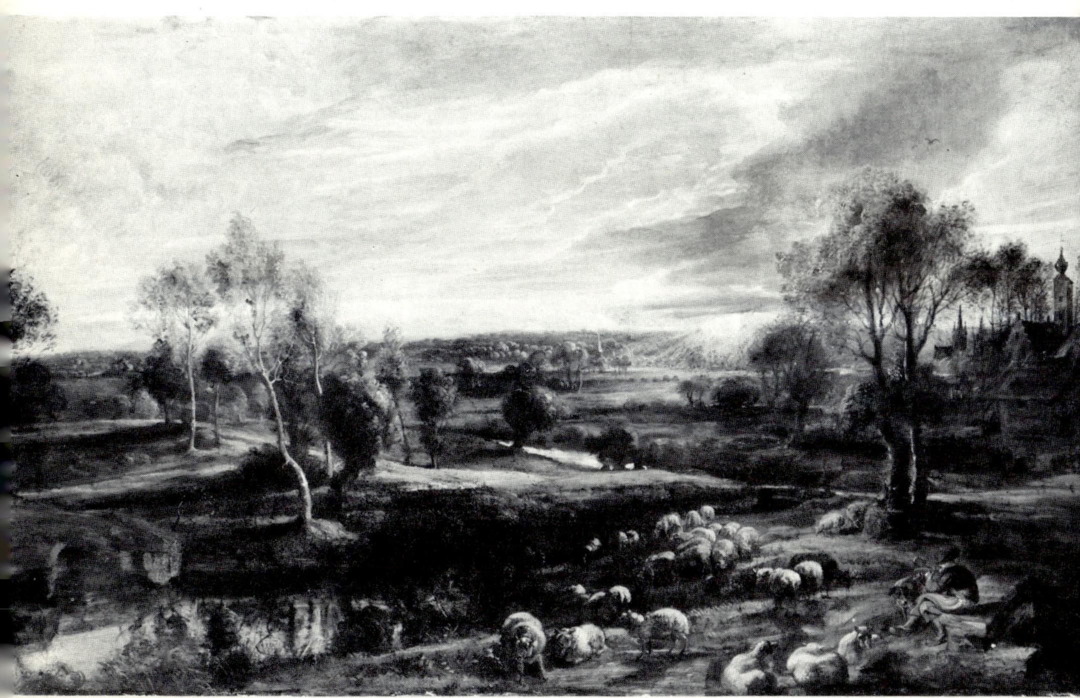

NOTE ON SOURCES

The basic source for the correspondence of Rubens is *Correspondance de Rubens et documents épistolaires concernant sa vie et ses œuvres* edited by Charles Ruelens and Max Rooses (6 volumes, Antwerp 1887–1909). The admirable translation of *The Letters of Peter Paul Rubens* by Ruth Saunders Magurn (Cambridge, Mass., 1955) contains all his known letters including ten never before published and a full apparatus of notes. As long ago as 1859 appeared the pioneer publication by W. Noel Sainsbury of *Original Unpublished Papers illustrative of the life of Sir Peter Paul Rubens as an artist and a diplomatist* (London 1859), which is particularly valuable for his diplomacy and especially the English mission; the documents in question are preserved among the State Papers in the Public Record Office.

LIST OF ILLUSTRATIONS

21 Part of a letter from Rubens to Sir Dudley
Carleton, dated 26 May 1618, Antwerp.
Public Record Office, London.

22 Michiel van Miereveldt: *Sir Dudley
Carleton. Canvas, c. 1620. National Portrait
Gallery, London.*

23 Philippe de Champaigne: *Triple portrait
of Cardinal Richelieu. Canvas, c. 1640.
National Gallery, London.*

24 Rubens: *Equestrian portrait of the Duke of
Buckingham.* Canvas, 1625. Formerly Earl
of Jersey, now destroyed. Photo Courtauld
Institute, London.

25 *The Infanta Isabella in the habit of a nun.*
Engraving by Pontius after Rubens, 1625.
British Library, London. Photo John
Freeman.

26 Rubens: *The Marquis Ambrogio Spinola.*
Canvas, *c. 1629. St Louis Art Museum.*

27 Velasquez: *The Surrender of Breda.* Canvas,
c. 1634–35. Prado, Madrid. Photo Mas.

28 Van Dyck: *Self-portrait.* Canvas, *c.* 1621–
22. *Alte Pinakothek, Munich.*

29 Van Dyck: *Virgin and Child adored by the
Abbé Scaglia. Canvas, c. 1634. National
Gallery, London.*

30 Van Dyck: *Equestrian portrait of Charles I
(detail). Canvas, c. 1638. National Gallery,
London.*

31 Gerard Honthorst: *Christ before Caiaphas.*
Canvas, *c. 1617. National Gallery, London.*

32 Velasquez: *Equestrian portrait of Count
Olivares* Canvas, *c.* 1634. Prado, Madrid.
Photo Mas.

33 Rubens: *Philip IV.* Canvas, *c.* 1628–29.
Alte Pinakothek, Munich.

34 Rubens: *Union of England and Scotland.*
Part of the Banqueting House ceiling.
Canvas, *c.* 1634. Banqueting House,
Whitehall, London. Photo Department
of the Environment.

35 Anon: *Sir Francis Cottington.* Canvas,
1634. *National Portrait Gallery, London.*

36 Studio of Rubens: *The Gerbier family.*
Canvas. *Royal Collection.* Reproduced by
gracious permission of Her Majesty the
Queen.

37 Rubens: *Allegory of Peace and War.* Canvas,
1629. *National Gallery, London.*

38 Rubens: *St George and the Dragon.* Canvas,
probably begun in 1630. *Royal Collection.*
Reproduced by gracious permission of
Her Majesty the Queen.

39 Rubens: *Hélène Fourment in her wedding
dress.* Panel, 1630. *Alte Pinakothek, Munich.*

40 Rubens: *Hélène Fourment with her children.*
Canvas, *c.* 1636. Louvre, Paris. Photo
Giraudon.

41 Rubens: *The artist with Hélène Fourment
and his son Nicholas, walking in their garden
in Antwerp.* Panel, *c.* 1631. *Alte Pinakothek,
Munich.*

42 Rubens: *Autumn landscape with a view of
the Château de Steen.* Panel, *c.* 1636.
National Gallery, London.

43 Rubens: *Self-portrait.* Canvas, 1638–40.
Kunsthistorisches Museum, Vienna.

44 Rubens's house, Antwerp. Photo ACL.
Copyright Rubenshuis.

45 Rubens's house, Antwerp. Interior. Photo
Jean de Maeyer. Copyright Rubenshuis.

46 Rubens: *Meeting of Cardinal-Infante
Ferdinand and Ferdinand, King of Hungary,
at the Battle of Nördlingen, 2 September 1634.*
Canvas, 1635. *Kunsthistorisches Museum,
Vienna.*

47 Rubens: *Cardinal-Infante Ferdinand.*
Canvas, 1635. *Kunsthistorisches Museum,
Vienna.*

48 Front face of the Arch of Ferdinand.
Etching by T. van Thulden for Gervasius's
Pompa introitus Ferdinandi. (Antwerp,
1641–42.)

49 Rubens: *Landscape with a shepherd and his
flock.* Panel, *c.* 1638. *National Gallery,
London.*